Our Conversion Experience

Todd Malkasian

Dedication

This book is dedicated to my great God Jesus, who spared my soul, and my wonderful wife Joyce. Thank you for your patience and support, as I worked on this project.

Acknowledgments

Thank you to Pastor Kenneth Bow, Dr. Dean Anderson, and my wife Joyce for taking time to review this book and provide some helpful editorial recommendations.

Table of Contents

__Foreword__

Regarding Todd Malkasian, I had the pleasure of being his pastor for many years. I can truly say that I have never known a more honest or sincere individual. All the years that I have known him, he has been a wonderful example of a true Christian, manifesting all of the fruits of the Spirit found in Galatians 5:22-23. It was very special to me to be involved in him being ordained into the ministry and to be asked to set on the church board of the church that he founded & pastored for many years. He has always been a very dedicated student of the Word of God and in this book you will find a gold mine of truth.

Rev. Jerry Green
Porter, Texas

The first time I met Rev. Todd Malkasian, I was evangelizing and he was pastoring a church in Sturtevant, WI. They were in the process of converting an industrial building that housed cranes into a church complex. I remember walking into what would be the current 275-seat sanctuary and thinking, "What a monumental task!"

Today, because of this man's vision and sacrifice, there is a beautiful church building including a sanctuary, parsonage, evangelist quarters, fellowship hall, school, and over 1.5 acres of prime property in Sturtevant, WI. When he called to ask me to pastor this church, I was humbled and grateful to be a part of this man and his wife's burden and sacrifice at Crossroads Apostolic Church.

He is a man that has made the kingdom of God his life. He is continuing to bless others with this book. You will see God's care and love as he shares his conversion experience.

Pastor Vaughn Pearson
Crossroads Apostolic Church, Sturtevant, WI

Preface

Prior to being invited to a United Pentecostal Church when I was twenty-five years old, I was *completely ignorant* to the New Testament plan of salvation preached by the Apostle Peter in the second chapter of the book of Acts:

> *"Then Peter said unto them, Repent, and be baptized every one of you in the name of Jesus Christ for the remission of sins, and ye shall receive the gift of the Holy Ghost" (Acts 2:38).*

I did not realize that the **exact same New Testament salvation experience** that the Apostle Peter, the Apostle Paul, and others received (and preached about) is *exactly* what God wants for **everyone** today.

I am writing this book in an effort to share *my conversion experience* with others. Some of my personal history and experiences are included to help you understand my background. I have tried to give a biblical explanation of *our conversion experience* along with some of my feelings and actions both *prior to* and *after* being converted.

Ever since becoming a member of God's New Testament Church, I have had such a deep love, not only for God, but for His cause. God has been so so very good to me. I love being in His Church. No words can ever properly express the thanks that I have to God for sparing my soul. My prayer is that this book will somehow help reach others with the precious truth that I have been blessed to receive and experience.

Part A: My Conversion Experience

When I was five years old, my mom died of breast cancer. When I was seven years old, my dad remarried. My dad was Lutheran and my mom was Catholic. We normally went to a church service every Sunday morning, unless we were on vacation or out of town. We usually alternated going to a Lutheran or Catholic Sunday-morning church service each week. When I was about fourteen years old, I went through confirmation classes and was confirmed at the Lutheran church that we were attending. I was given a Bible and started to take communion at this Lutheran church, which normally was given once a month. Although I attended hundreds of Catholic church services while growing up, I never took communion in a Catholic church.

My Lutheran or Catholic church service experiences usually consisted of: listening to someone read Bible verses, singing hymns, listening to announcements, giving an offering and greeting each another, quietly listening while the pastor or priest gave his sermon, taking communion, and having a dismissal prayer. We would sing hymns together as a congregation with everyone remaining in their pew. During the offering, I remember singing in some Lutheran church services: *"Create in me a clean heart, O God; and renew a right spirit within me. Cast me not away from thy presence; and take not thy holy spirit from me. Restore unto me the joy of thy salvation; and uphold me with thy free spirit" (Psalm 51:10-12).* Whenever anyone read a passage from the Bible or gave a sermon, everybody in the congregation was usually quiet. The Lutheran church service normally ended with the pastor saying a dismissal prayer and then blessing the congregation by saying: *"The LORD bless thee, and keep thee: The LORD make his face shine upon thee, and be gracious unto thee: The LORD lift up his countenance upon thee, and give thee peace" (Numbers 6:24-26).* Then the Lutheran pastor would say, "In the name of the Father, and of the Son, and of the Holy Spirit. Amen." The Lutheran pastor would then step down from the platform at the front of the church, walk down the center aisle to

1

the back of the church, and greet all of the congregation as we exited the church.

I graduated from Nicolet High School in Milwaukee, Wisconsin in May of 1978 and went to the US Naval Academy in Annapolis, Maryland in June of 1978. I brought my Bible with me to college, but I did not read it very often. While in college, I would attend a church service periodically if someone invited me, but I was not a consistent church-goer or member of any church.

I graduated from the US Naval Academy in May of 1982 and was commissioned as an officer in the U.S. Navy upon graduation. I went to West Germany as an exchange student with a group from the US Naval Academy for about a month immediately following graduation. I then went to: (a) Nuclear Power School in Orlando, Florida from July 1982 to December 1982, (b) Nuclear Prototype School in Ballston Spa, New York from January 1983 to June 1983, and (c) Surface Warfare Officers School in Coronado, California from July 1983 to November 1983. I then reported for duty on the USS Long Beach (CGN-9) and we went on a seven-month Indian Ocean and Western Pacific cruise from January of 1984 until August of 1984. We then went to Puget Sound Naval Shipyard in Bremerton, Washington from October of 1984 until October of 1985.

In the summer of 1985, while in Bremerton, Washington, I was invited by Roger Roth to go to his church. He invited me to the Granary Church, part of the United Pentecostal Church organization, pastored by Reverend Keith Painter. It was something that I had never experienced before. Although I had been in hundreds of church services, I had never witnessed anyone in a church service worship God with such enthusiasm or excitement. As the church service began and they started playing music and singing, someone would get out of their seat and jump up and down, or dance, or shout, or run around the church. I met many of these people before or after the service and they were all very kind and friendly. I had also never experienced someone preaching in such a powerful way. When the pastor or another minister preached or taught, many people responded in some way. Some people in the church service would periodically get up out of their seat and clap their hands or raise their hands. Others would shout "Amen!" or some other words of affirmation. The actions and words of these people showed that they agreed with what was being preached. At the end of the church service, while someone played music and sang songs, they would have "an altar call" and invite everyone to come up front to pray at the altar.

I had never witnessed "an altar call" in any of the Lutheran or Catholic church services that I had attended. The only altar call that I ever remember experiencing was at a Billy Graham crusade in Milwaukee, Wisconsin. When I was nineteen years old, while home from college, my Grandma Zastrow took me to this crusade. At the end of the crusade, they invited everyone to come down to the front to pray and "accept Jesus as their personal Savior." I believed that Jesus Christ was the Son of God. I believed that Jesus Christ died for our sins, was buried, and rose from the dead the third day. However, I never remembered being asked if I would "accept Jesus as my personal Savior." I remember going to the front and "accepting Jesus as my personal Savior," but I did not really feel a big change in my life.

Looking back, I do believe that God honored the fact that I got out of my seat and went to the front to "accept Jesus as my personal Savior" during that Billy Graham crusade. When I was twenty-one years old, after attending a home Navy football game on a Saturday in Annapolis, Maryland, I drove my car with four classmates to Atlantic City, New Jersey. We gambled all night long. We decided to drive back to the Naval Academy on Sunday morning, but I fell asleep at the wheel. The car that I was driving swerved to the right and crashed into two mailboxes, breaking the windshield in the car. But God spared my life and the lives of my four friends in the car with me! I thanked God over and over for sparing my life and the lives of my four friends.

After attending the Granary Church for several months, I went through a Bible study during the summer of 1985 and I saw my need to be baptized in the name of Jesus by full immersion in water. As a Lutheran, I believed that the Bible was the Word of God. I had been baptized as an infant in a Lutheran church when I was three-months old. However, they showed me in the Bible that we must believe in the death, burial, and resurrection of Jesus Christ *before* we are baptized. An innocent infant does not really understand or know what they are doing when they are baptized. Before I was baptized, I remember that the following Scripture really got my attention: *"Neither is there salvation in any other: for there is none other name under heaven given among men, whereby we must be saved" (Acts 4:12)*.

I was baptized in the name of Jesus in Puget Sound on September 1st, 1985 on a Sunday night after church. The ship that I was assigned to, the USS Long Beach (CGN-9), left Bremerton, Washington in October of 1985 and returned to San Diego, California.

While in San Diego, I was relieved of my duties as a division officer and given time to study for my Nuclear Engineer's exam. Although I had felt good and clean after being baptized in Jesus' name, I still had a deep hunger for God that had not yet been satisfied. While in San Diego, I would go on long walks, listening to Christian radio programs like "Unshackled," but still felt *very empty* on the inside. I had met people in Bremerton, Washington that had received the gift of the Holy Ghost with the initial outward evidence of speaking in other tongues (languages) as the Spirit of God gave them utterance. I had heard preaching and teaching from the Bible about people that had received the gift of the Holy Ghost. However, it was still something so *completely foreign* to me, so I still had my doubts. Was this experience for me?

I passed my oral and written Nuclear Engineer's exam, given by Naval Reactors in Washington DC, in February of 1986. I received orders to return to Bremerton, Washington in March of 1986 and resumed attending church services at the Granary Church in Bremerton, Washington.

While in pre-service church prayer, I received the baptism of the Holy Ghost in April of 1986, speaking in other tongues as the Spirit of God gave me utterance!! When I received the gift of the Holy Ghost, there was something in my innermost being that cried out saying "**This is it**!" It is something that I had been searching for my whole life, but never realized was available to me or anyone else. I had never before experienced such a *fullness* of the presence of God in my inner man.

In the days that followed this experience of receiving the gift of the Holy Ghost, I realized that something bigger than me, the Spirit of Jesus Christ, was living inside of me. It was not just something that I experienced *one time*, but instead, it was something that put such a FIRE inside of me that it made me want to "**SHOUT UNTO GOD WITH A VOICE OF TRIUMPH!**"

Looking back, I am not really sure why it took me such a long time to receive the gift of the Holy Ghost. I know that it was *completely different* from anything that I had ever been taught by any other church before coming to the Granary Church. I often felt uncomfortable when people at the Granary Church would ask me "Have you received the Holy Ghost?" and I would say "No." However, I thank God that instead of comforting me where I was in the salvation process, they encouraged me to complete the process.

Prior to receiving the baptism of the Holy Ghost, I never felt compelled or an inner prompting to tell someone about *my conversion experience*, because I had never really had one. While growing up, I learned many things regarding stories in the Bible and the life of Jesus Christ. However, I had never met someone that had been baptized in water in the name of Jesus *or* claimed they had spoken in other tongues as the Spirit of God gave them utterance, until attending the Granary Church in 1985.

Since taking on the name of Jesus in water baptism and being filled with the Holy Ghost when I was twenty-five years old, many changes have taken place in my life. I am writing this book in an effort to share *my conversion experience* and give a biblical explanation of what happened to me.

Part B: A Biblical Explanation of Our Conversion Experience

1 - The Authority of the Bible

The Word of God

"All scripture is given by inspiration of God, and is profitable for doctrine, for reproof, for correction, for instruction in righteousness" (2 Timothy 3:16).

The words "All scripture is given by inspiration of God" (2 Timothy 3:16, KJV) are translated as "Every Scripture is God-breathed (given by His inspiration)" (AMPCE). In 2 Timothy 3:16, the words "given by inspiration of God" come from the Greek word *theopneustos*, which means "divinely breathed in" or "God-breathed" (AMPCE). Although there were different men that wrote the Bible, God is the Author of *all* Scripture. All prophecy of the Scripture came from God:

> *"No prophecy of the scripture is of any private interpretation. For the prophecy came not in old time by the will of man: but holy men of God spake as they were moved by the Holy Ghost" (2 Peter 1:20-21). "For prophecy never had its origin in the will of man, but men spoke from God as they were carried along by the Holy Spirit" (2 Peter 1:21, NIV).*

The Word of God is forever settled and will never change: *"For ever, O LORD, thy word is settled in heaven" (Psalm 119:89).* Jesus said, *"For verily I say unto you, Till heaven and earth pass, one jot or one tittle shall in no wise pass from the law, till all be fulfilled" (Matthew 5:18).* We do not have authority to add, take away, or change any part of the Scriptures:

> *"What thing soever I command you, observe to do it: thou shalt not add thereto, nor diminish from it" (Deuteronomy 12:32).*

> *"Every word of God is pure...Add thou not unto his words, lest he reprove thee, and thou be found a liar" (Proverbs 30:5-6).*

"For I testify unto every man that heareth the words of the prophecy of this book, If any man shall add unto these things, God shall add unto him the plagues that are written in this book: And if any man shall take away from the words of the book of this prophecy, God shall take away his part out of the book of life, and out of the holy city, and from the things which are written in this book. He which testifieth these things saith, Surely I come quickly. Amen. Even so, come, Lord Jesus" (Revelation 22:18-20).

Judgment Day

We shall all someday stand before God in judgment, either as a *saved* (1 Corinthians 1:18; 15:2) or *lost* (Matthew 16:26; 2 Corinthians 4:3) individual. God will use His Word to judge us:

Jesus said, *"He that rejecteth me, and receiveth not my words, hath one that judgeth him: the word that I have spoken, the same shall judge him in the last day" (John 12:48).*

Paul wrote, *"The righteous judgment of God; Who will render to every man according to his deeds...In the day when God shall judge the secrets of men by Jesus Christ according to my gospel" (Romans 2:5-6, 16).*

"And as it is appointed unto men once to die, but after this the judgment" (Hebrews 9:27).

"For we must all appear before the judgment seat of Christ; that every one may receive the things done in his body, according to that he hath done, whether it be good or bad" (2 Corinthians 5:10).

"And I saw a great white throne, and him that sat on it, from whose face the earth and the heaven fled away; and there was found no place for them. And I saw the dead, small and great, stand before God; and the books were opened: and another book was opened, which is the book of life: and the dead were judged out of those things which were written in the books, according to their works. And the sea gave up the dead which were in it; and death and hell delivered up the dead which were in them: and they were judged every man according to

their works. And death and hell were cast into the lake of fire. This is the second death. And whosoever was not found written in the book of life was cast into the lake of fire" *(Revelation 20:11-15).*

In Revelation 20:11-15, two books are mentioned:
1. The "books" (a record or account of each person's life).
2. The "book of life" (Philippians 4:3; Revelation 3:5; 13:8; 17:8; 22:19) or "Lamb's book of life" (Revelation 21:27). Anyone who does not have their name written in the Lamb's book of life will be cast into the lake of fire.

Divisions of the New Testament

"Study to shew thyself approved unto God, a workman that needeth not to be ashamed, rightly dividing the word of truth" *(2 Timothy 2:15).*

The words "rightly dividing" (2 Timothy 2:15, KJV) are translated as "correctly handles" (NIV). We must study and "rightly divide" or "correctly handle" the Word of God so that we are not ashamed when we stand before God to be judged. The divisions of the New Testament are as follows:

1. **Four Gospels (Matthew, Mark, Luke, John)**. The life of Jesus Christ, including (a) His birth, (b) His forerunner John the Baptist, (c) His earthly ministry of preaching, teaching, miracles, and the calling of His disciples, (d) His death, burial, and resurrection, and (e) the commissioning of His apostles and His ascension.
2. **Acts (of the Apostles)**. These acts included (a) Jesus Christ's commissioning of His apostles and His ascension, (b) the birth of the New Testament Church in Acts chapter 2, and (c) the acts of the apostles, including the preaching or teaching of the New Testament plan of salvation by the apostles to others.
3. **Epistles (Romans through Jude)**. Letters of instruction to churches or individuals in God's New Testament Church, which had previously obeyed the plan of salvation preached by the apostles in the book of Acts.
4. **Revelation**. A revelation of the identity of Jesus Christ, instruction to churches, and future events.

We Must Obey What the Apostles Preached

There are many Scriptures that say we must obey what Peter and the other apostles preached, in order for us to be *saved*. Jesus endorsed His disciples and said that we are to believe on Him through the words that He gave to His disciples. Jesus said:

"Sanctify them through thy truth: thy word is truth. As thou hast sent me into the world, even so have I also sent them into the world. And for their sakes I sanctify myself, that they also might be sanctified through the truth. Neither pray I for these alone, but for them also which shall believe on me through their word" (John 17:17-20).

The wall of the heavenly city of new Jerusalem (Hebrews 12:22; Revelation 3:12; 21:2), the ultimate destination of those that are saved (Revelation 21:27), has twelve foundations. In these foundations are the names of the twelve apostles of the Lamb:

"And the wall of the city had twelve foundations, and in them the names of the twelve apostles of the Lamb" (Revelation 21:14).

Why are the names of the twelve apostles in these foundations? Because they handled the Word of God properly by preaching and teaching the correct New Testament plan of salvation. Peter wrote:

"Seeing ye have purified your souls in obeying the truth ...Being born again, not of corruptible seed, but of incorruptible, by the word of God, which liveth and abideth for ever...the word of the Lord endureth for ever. And this is the word which by the gospel is preached unto you" (1 Peter 1:22-25).

Paul wrote:

"Take heed unto thyself, and unto the doctrine; continue in them: for in doing this thou shalt both save thyself, and them that hear thee" (1 Timothy 4:16).

The words "the doctrine" (1 Timothy 4:16, KJV) are translated as "[your] teaching" (AMPCE). Continuing in Paul's doctrine (teaching) will both save yourself and those that hear you.

10

Paul wrote:

"But if our gospel be hid, it is hid to them that are lost: In whom the god of this world hath blinded the minds of them which believe not, lest the light of the glorious gospel of Christ, who is the image of God, should shine unto them"
(2 Corinthians 4:3-4).

Paul wrote that those who do not obey the gospel of Jesus Christ shall be punished:

"And to you who are troubled rest with us, when the Lord Jesus shall be revealed from heaven with his mighty angels, In flaming fire taking vengeance on them that know not God, and that obey not the gospel of our Lord Jesus Christ: Who shall be punished with everlasting destruction from the presence of the Lord, and from the glory of his power; When he shall come to be glorified in his saints, and to be admired in all them that believe (because our testimony among you was believed) in that day" (2 Thessalonians 1:7-10).

Paul wrote that some people or an angel from heaven may pervert (change) the gospel that Peter and Paul preached in the book of Acts and preach "another gospel." However, Paul let us know that there is *no other gospel* besides the gospel that Peter and Paul preached in the book of Acts:

"I marvel that ye are so soon removed from him that called you into the grace of Christ unto another gospel: Which is not another; but there be some that trouble you, and would pervert the gospel of Christ. But though we, or an angel from heaven, preach any other gospel unto you than that which we have preached unto you, let him be accursed. As we said before, so say I now again, If any man preach any other gospel unto you than that ye have received, let him be accursed"
(Galatians 1:6-9).

2 - <u>Some Attributes of God</u>

The Word of God is our guide to understanding God. According to the Bible, *"God is a Spirit" (John 4:24)* and a spirit does not have flesh and bones (Luke 24:39). Before we can understand Jesus Christ of the New Testament, we must have a proper understanding of the one God of the Bible.

<u>God Is Omnipresent</u>

God is present everywhere at all times:

> *"Know therefore this day, and consider it in thine heart, that the LORD he is God **in heaven above, and upon the earth beneath: there is none else**" (Deuteronomy 4:39).*

> *"But will God in very deed dwell with men on the earth? Behold, **heaven and the heaven of heavens cannot contain thee**; how much less this house which I have built!" (2 Chronicles 6:18).*

> *"Whither shall I go from thy spirit? Or whither shall I flee from thy presence? If I ascend up into heaven, thou art there: if I make my bed in hell, behold, thou art there. If I take the wings of the morning, and dwell in the uttermost parts of the sea; Even there shall thy hand lead me, and thy right hand shall hold me" (Psalm 139:7-10).*

> *"The eyes of the LORD are **in every place**, beholding the evil and the good" (Proverbs 15:3).*

> *"Thus saith the LORD, The **heaven is my throne, and the earth is my footstool**" (Isaiah 66:1).*

> *"Am I a God at hand, saith the LORD, and not a God afar off? Can any hide himself in secret places that I shall not see him? saith the LORD. **Do not I fill heaven and earth?** saith the LORD" (Jeremiah 23:23-24).*

<u>God Is Invisible</u>

God may visibly manifest Himself in some way. For example, John the Baptist saw the Spirit of God descend *"in a bodily shape like a dove" (Luke 3:22)* when he baptized Jesus Christ (Matthew 3:16; Mark 1:9-10; John 1:32-34). However, normally God cannot be seen by our human eye:

> God told Moses, *"Thou canst not see my face: for there shall no man see me, and live" (Exodus 33:20).*

> *"**No man hath seen God at any time**" (John 1:18).*

> *"Now unto the King eternal, immortal, **invisible**, the only wise God, be honour and glory for ever and ever" (1 Timothy 1:17).*

> *"Who only hath immortality, dwelling in the light which no man can approach unto; **whom no man hath seen, nor can see**: to whom be honour and power everlasting. Amen" (1 Timothy 6:16).*

> By faith Moses *"forsook Egypt, not fearing the wrath of the king: for he endured, as seeing him who is **invisible**" (Hebrews 11:27).*

God Is Self-Existent and Eternal

God has existed "from everlasting" (Psalm 90:2) and will always exist. He never becomes weary (Isaiah 40:28) or sleeps (Psalm 121:4). He is immortal (1 Timothy 1:17) and cannot die:

> *"The **eternal** God is thy refuge, and underneath are the **everlasting** arms" (Deuteronomy 33:27).*

> *"The LORD shall reign **for ever and ever**" (Exodus 15:18).*

> *"LORD, thou hast been our dwelling place in all generations. Before the mountains were brought forth, or ever thou hadst formed the earth and the world, even **from everlasting to everlasting, thou art God**" (Psalm 90:1-2).*

> *"O my God...Of old hast thou laid the foundation of the earth: and the heavens are the work of thy hands. They shall perish, but thou shalt endure: yea, all of them shall wax old like a garment; as a vesture shalt thou change them, and they shall be changed: But thou art the same, and **thy years shall have no end**" (Psalm 102:24-27).*

14

*"Trust ye in the LORD **for ever**: for in the LORD JEHOVAH is **everlasting** strength" (Isaiah 26:4).*

*"Hast thou not known? hast thou not heard, that **the everlasting God**, the LORD, the Creator of the ends of the earth, fainteth not, neither is weary? there is no searching of his understanding" (Isaiah 40:28).*

God Is Omniscient

God knows the thoughts, desires, and motives of every individual. God declares the end from the beginning. God knows everything about everyone and all things, whether it be in the past, present, or future:

*"O LORD, thou hast searched me, and known me. Thou knowest my downsitting and mine uprising, **thou understandest my thought afar off**. Thou compassest my path and my lying down, and art acquainted with all my ways. For there is not a word in my tongue, but, lo, O LORD, thou knowest it altogether. Thou hast beset me behind and before, and laid thine hand upon me. Such knowledge is too wonderful for me; it is high, I cannot attain unto it" (Psalm 139:1-6).*

*"Great is our Lord, and of great power: **his understanding is infinite**" (Psalm 147:5).*

*"Remember the former things of old: for I am God, and there is none else; I am God, and there is none like me, **Declaring the end from the beginning**, and from ancient times the things that are not yet done, saying, My counsel shall stand, and I will do all my pleasure" (Isaiah 46:9-10).*

"Known unto God are all his works from the beginning of the world" (Acts 15:18).

"Neither is there any creature that is not manifest in his sight: but all things are naked and opened unto the eyes of him with whom we have to do" (Hebrews 4:13).

*"For if our heart condemn us, God is greater than our heart, and **knoweth all things**" (1 John 3:20).*

God Is Omnipotent

God has all power in heaven and in earth:

God told Abram, *"I am the **Almighty God"** (Genesis 17:1).*

God told Jacob, *"I am **God Almighty"** (Genesis 35:11).*

David said, *"Thine, O LORD, is the greatness, and **the power**, and the glory, and the victory, and the majesty: for all that is in the heaven and in the earth is thine; thine is the kingdom, O LORD, and **thou art exalted as head above all**. Both riches and honour come of thee, and **thou reignest over all; and in thine hand is power and might**; and in thine hand it is to make great, and to give strength unto all"* (1 Chronicles 29:11-12).

Jehoshaphat said, *"O LORD God of our fathers, art not thou God in heaven? and rulest not thou over all the kingdoms of the heathen? and **in thine hand is there not power and might, so that none is able to withstand thee?"** (2 Chronicles 20:6).*

*"Job answered the LORD, and said, I know that **thou canst do every thing**, and that no thought can be withholden from thee"* (Job 42:1-2).

God *"ruleth by his power for ever"* (Psalm 66:7).

Jeremiah said, *"Ah Lord GOD! Behold, thou hast made the heaven and the earth by thy great power and stretched out arm, and **there is nothing too hard for thee"*** (Jeremiah 32:17).

The LORD said, *"Yea, before the day was I am he; and **there is none that can deliver out of my hand**: I will work, and who shall let it?"* (Isaiah 43:13).

Jesus said, *"With God all things are possible"* (Matthew 19:26).

*"And I heard as it were the voice of a great multitude, and as the voice of many waters, and as the voice of mighty thunderings, saying, Alleluia: for the **Lord God omnipotent** reigneth"* (Revelation 19:6).

16

The One God of the Old Testament

In the Old Testament, there are various Hebrew words used for God or Lord. God said: `

> "*I am the LORD* [Hebrew: YHWH]*: that is my name: and my glory will I not give to another, neither my praise to graven images" (Isaiah 42:8).*

YHWH, God's name in the ancient Hebrew language, is defined by J. Strong as: "(The) self-Existent or Eternal; Jehovah, Jewish national name of God." W. E. Vine explains the word "Lord" in *Vine's Expository Dictionary of OT Words*:

> The Tetragrammaton YHWH appears without its own vowels, and its exact pronunciation is debated (Jehovah, Yehovah, Jahweh, Yahweh). The Hebrew text does insert the vowels for `adonay, and Jewish students and scholars read `adonay whenever they see the Tetragrammaton. This use of the word occurs 6,828 times. The word appears in every period of biblical Hebrew.
>
> The divine name YHWH appears only in the Bible. Its precise meaning is much debated. God chose it as His personal name by which He related specifically to His chosen or covenant people. Its first appearance in the biblical record is Gen 2:4: "These are the generations of the heavens and of the earth when they were created, in the day that the Lord God made the earth and the heavens." Apparently Adam knew Him by this personal or covenantal name from the beginning, since Seth both called his son Enosh (i.e., man as a weak and dependent creature) and began (along with all other pious persons) to call upon (formally worship) the name of YHWH, "the Lord" (Gen 4:26).[1]

In the KJV Bible, God's name YHWH is translated as:

1. "JEHOVAH" (all capital letters) in four verses (Exodus 6:3; Psalm 83:18; Isaiah 12:2; 26:4).
2. "Jehovah" in the compound names "Jehovah-jireh"(Genesis 22:14),"Jehovah-nissi" (Exodus 17:15), and "Jehovah-shalom" (Judges 6:24).
3. "GOD" (all capital letters) in some verses.

17

4. "LORD" (all capital letters) in many verses.

Here are some examples of YHWH being translated as "LORD" or "GOD":

> *"These are the generations of the heavens and of the earth when they were created, in the day that the LORD* [Hebrew: YHWH] *God made the earth and the heavens"*
> *(Genesis 2:4).*

> *"And GOD* [Hebrew: YHWH] *saw that the wickedness of man was great in the earth, and that every imagination of the thoughts of his heart was only evil continually"*
> *(Genesis 6:5).*

> *"Thrice in the year shall all your men children appear before the Lord GOD* [Hebrew: YHWH], *the God of Israel"*
> *(Exodus 34:23).*

The Hebrew word YHWH, God's name in the Old Testament, can be translated into English as "Yahweh" or "Jehovah." In this book, we will use Jehovah, since that is what the KJV Bible uses. Jehovah is the one God of the Old Testament:

> *"Hear, O Israel: The LORD our God is one LORD"*
> *(Deuteronomy 6:4).*

> *"Hear, O Israel: The LORD our God, **the LORD is one**!"*
> *(Deuteronomy 6:4, NKJV).*

There Is Only One God

There is only one God:

> *"There is none other God but one" (1 Corinthians 8:4).*

> *"Now a mediator is not a mediator of one, but **God is one**"*
> *(Galatians 3:20).*

> *"For **there is one God**" (1 Timothy 2:5).*

> *"Thou believest that **there is one God**; thou doest well: the devils also believe, and tremble" (James 2:19).*

There Is No God or Savior Beside Jehovah

There is no God or Savior beside the one true God, Jehovah, who is the first and the last:

> *"Unto thee it was shewed, that thou mightest know that the LORD he is God;* ***there is none else beside him****...the LORD he is God in heaven above, and upon the earth beneath:* ***there is none else****" (Deuteronomy 4:35, 39).*

> *"Ye are my witnesses, saith the LORD, and my servant whom I have chosen: that ye may know and believe me, and understand that I am he:* ***before me there was no God formed, neither shall there be after me****. I, even I, am the LORD; and* ***beside me there is no saviour****" (Isaiah 43:10-11).*

> *"Thus saith the LORD the King of Israel, and his redeemer the LORD of hosts; I am the first, and I am the last; and* ***beside me there is no God****...**Is there a God beside me? Yea, there is no God; I know not any****" (Isaiah 44:6, 8).*

> *"(5) I am the LORD, and* ***there is none else, there is no God beside me****...(6)* ***there is none beside me****. I am the LORD, and* ***there is none else****...(18) For thus saith the LORD that created the heavens; God himself that formed the earth and made it...I am the LORD; and* ***there is none else****...(21) and* ***there is no God else beside me; a just God and a Saviour; there is none beside me****. (22) Look unto me, and be ye saved, all the ends of the earth: for I am God, and* ***there is none else****" (Isaiah 45:5, 6, 18, 21, 22).*

Jehovah Is Our Creator

Jehovah created us and everything in the world by Himself:

> *"Thou, even thou, art LORD* ***alone****; thou hast made heaven, the heaven of heavens, with all their host, the earth, and all things that are therein, the seas, and all that is therein, and thou preservest them all; and the host of heaven worshippeth thee" (Nehemiah 9:6).*

> *"By the word of the LORD were the heavens made; and all the host of them by the breath of his mouth" (Psalm 33:6).*

"Thus saith God the LORD, he that created the heavens, and stretched them out; he that spread forth the earth, and that which cometh out of it; he that giveth breath unto the people upon it, and spirit to them that walk therein" (Isaiah 42:5).

*"Thus saith the LORD, thy redeemer, and he that formed thee from the womb, I am the LORD that maketh all things; that stretcheth forth the heavens **alone**; that spreadeth abroad the earth **by myself**"* (Isaiah 44:24).

"Have we not all one father? Hath not one God created us?" (Malachi 2:10).

Jehovah Owns Everything and Everyone

Jehovah owns us and everything in the world:

"Behold, the heaven and the heaven of heavens is the LORD's thy God, the earth also, with all that therein is" (Deuteronomy 10:14).

The LORD told Moses, *"All the earth is mine"* (Exodus 19:5).

"The earth is the LORD's, and the fulness thereof; the world, and they that dwell therein" (Psalm 24:1).

The LORD (Job 40:6) said to Job, *"Whatsoever is under the whole heaven is mine"* (Job 41:11).

Jehovah Forgives Our Sins

Jehovah forgives our sins:

*"Bless the LORD, O my soul, and forget not all his benefits: **Who forgiveth all thine iniquities**; who healeth all thy diseases...**As far as the east is from the west, so far hath he removed our transgressions from us**"* (Psalm 103:2-3, 12).

*"Thus saith the LORD...I, even I, am he that **blotteth out thy transgressions for mine own sake, and will not remember thy sins**"* (Isaiah 43:16, 25).

*"Saith the LORD; for **I will forgive their iniquity, and I will remember their sin no more**"* (Jeremiah 31:34).

Jehovah's Character and Power

Although God never changes (Malachi 3:6), different aspects of His character and power were witnessed by various people throughout the Old Testament. Although Abraham had built *"an altar unto the LORD" (Genesis 12:7)*, called on *"the name of the LORD" (Genesis 12:8, 13:4)*, *"believed in the LORD" (Genesis 15:6)*, and made a covenant with *"the LORD" (Genesis 15:18)*, Abraham had not yet seen certain aspects of God's character. After God saw that Abraham obeyed His command to sacrifice his only son Isaac, God provided a ram to be sacrificed instead of Isaac:

> *"And Abraham stretched forth his hand, and took the knife to slay his son. And the angel of the LORD called unto him out of heaven, and said, Abraham, Abraham: and he said, Here am I. And he said, Lay not thine hand upon the lad, neither do thou any thing unto him: for now I know that thou fearest God, seeing thou hast not withheld thy son, thine only son from me. And Abraham lifted up his eyes, and looked, and behold behind him a ram caught in a thicket by his horns: and Abraham went and took the ram, and offered him up for a burnt offering in the stead of his son. And Abraham called the name of that place Jehovah-jireh: as it is said to this day, In the mount of the LORD it shall be seen"*
> *(Genesis 22:10-14).*

In this instance, God revealed Himself to Abraham as "Jehovah-jireh" (Genesis 22:14), which is defined as: "Jehovah will see (to it)."

When Moses was about eighty years old, God spoke to him from a burning bush and called him to lead the children of Israel out of Egypt (Exodus 3:1-22). God made Himself known to Moses as "JEHOVAH" (Exodus 6:3), the God that delivers out of Egyptian bondage and fulfills His promise to give the land of Canaan to the children of Israel (Exodus 6:1-8). God demonstrated His great power, *as never seen before*, by exposing and defeating the various false gods of Egypt with ten different plagues (Exodus chapters 7 to 13).

After God delivered the children of Israel out of Egyptian bondage, He did the following for them (Deuteronomy 8:2-4, 14-16):

1. Led them as a pillar of a cloud during the day and as a pillar of fire during the night throughout all their journeys (Exodus 13:21-22; 40:38; Numbers 9:15-23).
2. Gave them permanent deliverance from their Egyptian enemies, so that they would *"see them again no more for ever" (Exodus 14:13)*. God parted the waters of the Red Sea for the children of Israel to walk through safely, and then closed the waters of the Red Sea so that Pharaoh and his pursuing army drowned (Exodus 14:15-31).
3. Fed them with "manna" ("bread") from heaven (John 6:31; Psalm 78:24) for forty years until they reached the border of Canaan (Exodus 16:35; Joshua 5:12). The manna was *"a small round thing" (Exodus 16:14)* that was like *"white coriander seed" (Exodus 16:31; NKJV)*. The manna tasted *"like wafers made with honey" (Exodus 16:31)* or *"pastry prepared with oil" (Numbers 11:8, NKJV)*.
4. Gave them water to drink. God miraculously (a) turned the bitter waters of Marah sweet (Exodus 15:22-26), (b) brought water out of a rock at Horeb after Moses struck it with his rod (Exodus 17:1-7), and (c) brought water out of a rock in Kadesh, in spite of Moses striking the rock instead of speaking to it (Numbers 20:1-13).
5. Had their clothes and shoes *not* wear out during their forty-year journey (Deuteronomy 8:4; Nehemiah 9:21).

As Moses and the nation of Israel journeyed further away from Egypt, God gave the Israelites victory when the people of Amalek fought against them (Exodus 17:8-13). God also proclaimed that He would give the Israelites victory over the Amalekites in the future (Exodus 17:14). God showed Himself to the Israelites as the God that will give them victory when they fight against their foes. Moses built an altar and named it "Jehovah-nissi" (Exodus 17:15), which means: "Jehovah (is) my banner."

An angel of the LORD appeared to Gideon and told him: *"The LORD is with thee, thou mighty man of valour" (Judges 6:12).* Then the LORD said to Gideon: *"Go in this thy might, and thou shalt save Israel from the hand of the Midianites: have not I sent thee?...Surely I will be with thee, and thou shalt smite the Midianites as one man...Peace be unto thee; fear not: thou shalt not die" (Judges 6:14, 16, 23).* God revealed Himself to Gideon as the God that will give him an inner "peace" even when fighting enemy forces. *"Then Gideon built an altar there unto the LORD, and called it Jehovah-shalom" (Judges 6:24).* "Jehovah-shalom" (Judges 6:24) means: "Jehovah (is) peace."

In the New Testament, God revealed Himself as Jehovah our Savior, when He manifested Himself in the flesh to save us (Isaiah 35:4-6; 40:3-5; Matthew 1:21; 11:3-5; Luke 7:20-22; 1 Timothy 3:16).

3 - Jesus Christ

The Birth of Jesus Christ

The virgin Mary was told by the angel Gabriel that the child conceived in her womb should be called the "Son of God" (Luke 1:35). Both Mary and her espoused husband Joseph were told by angels that Mary's Son should be called "JESUS" (Luke 1:30-31; 2:21; Matthew 1:18-25). W.E. Vine states that the name "Jesus" (Greek: *Iesous*):

> Is a transliteration of the Heb. "Joshua," meaning "Jehovah is salvation," i.e., "is the Savior."[2]

When did Jehovah, the one God of the Old Testament, become our Savior? Jehovah became our Savior when the Holy Ghost overshadowed the virgin Mary (Isaiah 7:14; 9:6-7; Matthew 1:18, 20-23; Luke 1:31-35) and Jesus Christ, the Savior of the world (John 4:42), was born (Luke 2:11).

As a man, Jesus of Nazareth was "anointed" by God (Isaiah 61:1-2; Luke 4:18-19; Acts 4:27, 10:38; Hebrews 1:9). The word "Christ" (Greek: *Christos*) and the word "Messiah" (John 1:41; 4:25 from Daniel 9:25-26) both mean "the Anointed One"[3]: *"We have found (discovered) the Messiah! – which translated is the Christ (the Anointed One)" (John 1:41, AMPCE).* In the New Testament, since the title *Christ* and the name *Jesus* both refer to the same person, they are frequently used for Jesus Christ.

Jesus Christ was Emmanuel, God with us, when he was born of the virgin Mary (Isaiah 7:14; Matthew 1:21-23). Jesus Christ was both God (deity) and man (humanity). In His deity, He was David's God (Matthew 22:42-45; Mark 12:35-37) or "root" (Revelation 22:16). In his humanity, he was David's son (Luke 3:31; Acts 2:30; Romans 1:3; 2 Timothy 2:8) or "offspring" (Revelation 22:16). His deity has *always existed* (Micah 5:2), but his humanity *did not exist* prior to being miraculously conceived by the Holy Ghost in the womb of the virgin Mary (Galatians 4:4).

When Jesus Christ was born in Bethlehem, angels made a public announcement (Luke 2:8-20) and wise men came privately to worship Him (Micah 5:2; Matthew 2:1-11). The wise men presented gifts to this new born King of the Jews (Matthew 2:11).

25

The Baptism of Jesus Christ

A prophet named John the Baptist (Matthew 3:1; Luke 7:27-28) publicly declared that Jehovah (Isaiah 40:3-5; Malachi 3:1), the One God of the Old Testament (Deuteronomy 6:4), was coming inside of a sinless man (Matthew 3:3; Mark 1:2-3; Luke 3:4-6; John 1:23). Jesus Christ, a humble thirty-year old man (Luke 3:23) and the sacrificial Lamb of God (John 1:29; 1 Corinthians 5:7; 1 Peter 1:19), was washed by a descendant of the first Levitical high priest Aaron (1 Chronicles 24:10; Matthew 3:15; Luke 1:5, 13) when he was baptized by John the Baptist in the Jordan river.

At his baptism, Jesus Christ was publicly anointed and introduced by God. The Spirit of God, descending as a theophany in the form of a dove (Matthew 3:16; Mark 1:10; Luke 3:22), was a sign to John the Baptist that Jesus is the Son of God (John 1:31-34). The voice from heaven, saying: *"This is my beloved Son, in whom I am well pleased" (Matthew 3:17*; see also Mark 1:11; Luke 3:22), which also occurred at the transfiguration (Matthew 17:5; Mark 9:7; Luke 9:35) and triumphal entry of King Jesus (Zechariah 9:9; Matthew 21:5; Luke 19:38; John 12:28-30), was honor and glory from God (2 Peter 1:17-18) and for the people's sake (John 12:30).

Jesus Christ Was God Manifested in the Flesh

"And without controversy great is the mystery of godliness: God was manifest in the flesh" (1 Timothy 3:16). The "mystery of godliness" is that God **miraculously conceived and dwelt** in His Son, Jesus Christ, in the womb of the virgin Mary. We, as finite human beings, cannot fully comprehend how an infinite God can manifest Himself in a finite human being.

When God manifested Himself in Jesus Christ (John 1:10-11; 2 Corinthians 5:19), was heaven or the throne of God vacant? No, because God is an omnipresent Spirit (2 Chronicles 6:18). All of God in quality, not quantity, dwelt in Jesus Christ: *"For in him dwelleth all the fulness of the Godhead bodily. And ye are complete in him, which is the head of all principality and power" (Colossians 2:9-10).* Jesus Christ was not an ordinary man, for the Spirit of God (dwelling in him) empowered him to overcome all temptations and never sin.

26

Sometimes Jesus Christ spoke or acted as a man and other times He spoke or acted as God. As a man, Jesus Christ:

- Was born (Luke 2:11) with a body (Hebrews 10:5), soul (Matthew 26:38), spirit (Mark 2:8; 8:12; Luke 23:46), and sinless nature or flesh (1 John 3:5; 2 Corinthians 5:21).
- Grew in wisdom (Luke 2:52); learned obedience (Heb. 5:8).
- Became weary (John 4:6); slept (Matt. 8:24); was limited in power (John 5:19, 30; 14:10) and knowledge (Mark 13:32).
- Prayed (Matthew 14:23; Mark 1:35; Luke 5:16; 6:12; 9:28).
- Was tempted (Matthew 4:1-11; Hebrews 4:15).
- Lived a sinless life (Hebrews 4:15; 1 Peter 2:22).
- Wept (Luke 19:41; John 11:35).
- Served others (Matt. 20:26-28; Luke 22:26-27; John 13:14-15).
- Gave thanks (Matthew 26:27; Mark 14:23; Luke 22:17, 19).
- Submitted his human will to God's will (Matthew 26:39-44; Luke 22:42; Philippians 2:8); forgave others (Luke 23:34).
- Suffered (Luke 24:26; Heb. 2:9-10; 1 Peter 2:21-24; 3:18; 4:1).
- Was scourged (Matthew 27:26; Mark 15:15; John 19:1).
- Willingly died an extremely painful death by crucifixion for the sins of the world (John 10:15-18; 15:13; 18:11).

As God, Jesus:

- Existed from everlasting (Micah 5:2; John 8:58).
- Created all things (John 1:10; 1 Corinthians 8:6; Colossians 1:16-18; Hebrews 1:2, 10-12; Revelation 4:11).
- Forgave sins (Matthew 9:2-7; Mark 2:5-12; Luke 7:47-48).
- Calmed a storm (Matt. 8:23-27; Mark 4:37-41; Luke 8:23-25).
- Multiplied food to feed a multitude (Matthew 14:13-21; Mark 6:38-44; Luke 9:12-17; John 6:9-14).
- Healed people (Matthew 4:24; 8:3, 16; 15:30); raised the dead (Mark 5:41-42; Luke 7:14-15; John 11:43; 12:1, 9).
- Accepted worship (Matthew 8:2; 9:18; 14:33; 15:25; 28:9, 17; Mark 5:6; Luke 24:52; John 9:38); was worshipped by angels (Hebrews 1:6) and wise men (Matthew 2:11).
- Raised the body of Christ from the dead (John 2:19-21).
- Knew everything (John 2:24-25; 16:30; 18:4; 21:17; Colossians 2:3).

As a man, Jesus Christ said, *"My Father is greater than I"* *(John 14:28)*, signifying that His **deity** is greater than his **humanity**. However, as God, Jesus Christ was *"equal with God"* *(Philippians 2:6)*. Jesus Christ could say, *"He that hath seen me, hath seen the Father" (John 14:9)*, for he was *"the image of the invisible God" (Colossians 1:15)*.

As God, Jesus is an omnipresent invisible Spirit (Matthew 18:20; 28:20), Who is omnipotent (Matthew 28:18; Colossians 2:9-10; Revelation 1:8) and answers our prayers (John 14:13-14). As God, Jesus never becomes weary (Isaiah 40:28), and never sleeps (Psalm 121:4). As God, Jesus gives us spiritual "rest" (Isaiah 28:11-12; Matthew 11:28-30) and "living water" (John 7:37-39), when He baptizes us with the Holy Ghost (Matthew 3:11; Mark 1:8; Luke 3:16; John 1:33).

The term "Son of God" (Mark 1:1; Luke 1:35; John 1:34, 49; 20:31; Acts 8:37; 9:20; Romans 1:4; 2 Cor. 1:19; Gal. 2:20; Eph. 4:13; Heb. 4:14; 6:6; 7:3; 10:29; 1 John 3:8; 4:15; 5:5, 10, 12, 13, 20) is found throughout the New Testament, but the term "God the Son" is not found in the Bible. Jesus Christ **never referred to Himself as "God the Son,"** but instead, He referred to Himself as: (1) The "Son" (Mark 13:32), (2) The "Son of God" (John 3:18; 5:25; 9:35-37; 10:36; 11:4; Revelation 2:18), for God was his Father and dwelt in him (John 10:38; 14:10-11; 17:21), or (3) The "Son of man" (Matthew 8:20; 9:6; 12:8; 16:13; Mark 10:33; 13:26; Luke 9:56; John 3:13; 12:23), for Mary was his mother (Luke 2:7).

The Gospel of Jesus Christ

When Adam and Eve sinned in the garden of Eden by disobeying God (Genesis chapter 3), there was some *bad news*:
1. **Spiritual and physical death**. They died an immediate spiritual death by being separated from God, and they died an eventual physical death:

    *"But of the tree of the knowledge of good and evil, thou shalt not eat of it: for in the day that thou eatest thereof **thou shalt surely die" (Genesis 2:17).***

    "In the sweat of thy face shalt thou eat bread, till thou return unto the ground; for out of it wast thou taken: for

dust thou art, and unto dust shalt thou return"
(Genesis 3:19).

*"And all the days that Adam lived were nine hundred and thirty years: and **he died**" (Genesis 5:5).*

*"**The soul that sinneth, it shall die**" (Ezekiel 18:20).*

*"For **the wages of sin is death**" (Romans 6:23).*

2. **Curses**. Various curses were placed upon the serpent, women, and men (Genesis 3:14, 16-19).

3. **Inherited sinful nature**. All of their descendants, except for Jesus Christ, would be born into this world with a sinful nature:

   "Among whom also we all had our conversation in times past in the lusts of our flesh, fulfilling the desires of the flesh and of the mind; and were by nature the children of wrath, even as others" (Ephesians 2:3).

   *We "**are all under sin**; As it is written, There is none righteous, no, not one: There is none that understandeth, there is none that seeketh after God...That every mouth may be stopped, and all the world may become guilty before God...For **all have sinned, and come short of the glory of God**" (Romans 3:9-11, 19, 23).*

   *"Wherefore, as by one man sin entered into the world, and death by sin; and so death passed upon all men, for that **all have sinned**" (Romans 5:12).*

   *"For as **by one man's disobedience many were made sinners**, so by the obedience of one shall many be made righteous" (Romans 5:19).*

   *"For since **by man came death**, by man came also the resurrection of the dead. For **as in Adam all die**, even so in Christ shall all be made alive" (1 Corinthians 15:21-22).*

However, even in the midst of sharing this *bad news*, God had some *good news* and proclaimed His plan of salvation to the serpent: *"And I will put enmity between thee and the woman, and between thy seed and her seed; it shall bruise thy head, and thou shalt bruise his heel" (Genesis 3:15).* The word "it" (Gen. 3:15, KJV) is translated as "He" (NKJV). The word "seed" (Gen. 3:15, KJV) is translated as "offspring" (NIV).

29

W.E. Vine states that the word "gospel" (Greek: *euangelion*) can mean "the good news."[4] The *good news*, or the *gospel* of Jesus Christ, is that God made a way where there was no way! God's extreme hatred of sin and intense love for the sinner was displayed at the cross of Calvary. God provided a spotless Lamb to take away the sins of the world and reconcile all of us back to God. Jesus Christ not only recovered everything that Adam lost in the garden of Eden, but also made a way for us to be overcomers in this life.

Jesus Christ was born (Galatians 4:4) with a sinless nature or flesh (similar to the innocent flesh that Adam had before he sinned in the garden of Eden), for *"in him is no sin" (1 John 3:5)* and he *"knew no sin" (2 Corinthians 5:21)*. He never sinned, for he *"did no sin" (1 Peter 2:22)* and *"was in all points tempted like as we are, yet without sin" (Hebrews 4:15)*.

Jesus Christ willingly suffered for us (Luke 24:26; Hebrews 2:18; 5:8; 13:12; 1 Peter 2:21-23) and his sinless body was "broken" for us (1 Corinthians 11:24). He was "scourged" (Matthew 27:26; Mark 15:15; John 19:1, KJV) or "flogged" (NIV) by the Romans. The *Holman Christian Standard Bible* footnote on "flogged" (Matthew 27:26) states:

> Roman flogging was done with a whip made of leather strips embedded with pieces of bone or metal that brutally tore the flesh.[5]

The word "scourged" in Matthew 27:26 and Mark 15:15 is translated from the Greek word *phragelloo*. W. E. Vine explains the word *phragelloo*:

> Under the Roman method of "scourging," the person was stripped and tied in a bending posture to a pillar, or stretched on a frame. The "scourge" was made of leather thongs, weighted with sharp pieces of bone or lead, which tore the flesh of both the back and the breast.[6]

The flogging inflicted upon Jesus provided both *physical* and *spiritual* healing for us, for *"With his stripes we are healed" (Isaiah 53:5)* and *"By whose stripes, ye were healed" (1 Peter 2:24)*. His hands and feet were pierced (Psalm 22:16; John 20:25-27), his sinless blood was shed, and he died a torturous death by crucifixion at the "place of a skull" called Golgotha (Matthew 27:33; Mark 15:22; John 19:17) or Calvary (Luke 23:33). The death of Jesus Christ and the shedding of his innocent blood:

1. **Paid the price to redeem us to God and purchase our salvation.** Jesus Christ bought (1 Corinthians 6:19-20) or purchased His Church with His own blood:

    *"In whom we have **redemption through his blood**, the forgiveness of sins, according to the riches of his grace" (Ephesians 1:7).*

    *"Take heed therefore unto yourselves, and to all the flock, over the which the Holy Ghost hath made you overseers, to feed the **church of God**, which he hath **purchased with his own blood**" (Acts 20:28).*

    *"And from **Jesus Christ**, who is the faithful witness, and the first begotten of the dead, and the prince of the kings of the earth. Unto him that loved us, and **washed us from our sins in his own blood**" (Revelation 1:5).*

    *"(18) Forasmuch as ye know that ye were not **redeemed with corruptible things**, as silver and gold, from your vain conversation received by tradition from your fathers; (19) But with **the precious blood of Christ, as of a lamb without blemish and without spot**: (20) Who verily was foreordained before the foundation of the world, but was manifest in these last times for you" (1 Peter 1:18-20).*

    The word "redeemed" in 1 Peter 1:18 is translated from the Greek word *lutroo*. W.E. Vine states that *lutroo* means: "to release on receipt of ransom...to release by paying a ransom price."[7]

    *"And they sung a new song, saying, Thou art worthy to take the book, and to open the seals thereof: for **thou wast slain, and hast redeemed us to God by thy blood** out of every kindred, and tongue, and people, and nation" (Revelation 5:9).*

    The word "redeemed" (Revelation 5:9, KJV) is translated as "purchased" (NIV). The word "redeemed" in Revelation 5:9 is translated from the Greek word *agorazo*. Regarding the word *agorazo*, W. E. Vine states: "Figuratively Christ is spoken of as having bought His redeemed, making them His property at the price of His blood."[8]

As stated by the *Webster's 1913 Online Dictionary*, the word "redeem" can be defined as: "1. To purchase back; to regain possession of by payment of a stipulated price; to repurchase…3. To ransom, liberate, or rescue from captivity or bondage…by paying a price or ransom…4. to rescue and deliver from the bondage of sin and the penalties of God's violated law."[9]

2. **Provided a substitutionary sacrifice for each of us and our sins**. Jesus Christ was the Lamb of God that took away the sin of the world (John 1:29; 1 Peter 1:18-19):

   *"My little children, these things write I unto you, that ye sin not. And if any man sin, we have an advocate with the Father, Jesus Christ the righteous: And **he is the propitiation for our sins: and not for ours only, but also for the sins of the whole world**" (1 John 2:1-2).*

   *"In this is love: not that we loved God, but that He loved us and sent His Son to be **the propitiation (the atoning sacrifice) for our sins**" (1 John 4:10, AMPCE).*

   *"Who **his own self bare our sins in his own body** on the tree, that we, being dead to sins, should live unto righteousness" (1 Peter 2:24).*

   *"For Christ also **hath once suffered for sins**, the just for the unjust, that he might bring us to God" (1 Peter 3:18).*

   *"For **he hath made him to be sin for us, who knew no sin**; that we might be made the righteousness of God in him" (2 Corinthians 5:21).*

   "And walk in love, as Christ also hath loved us, and hath given himself for us an offering and a sacrifice to God for a sweetsmelling savour" (Ephesians 5:2).

   Jesus *"resisted unto blood, striving against sin" (Hebrews 12:4), "**put away sin by the sacrifice of himself**"*

(Hebrews 9:26), and *"**was once offered to bear the sins of many**" (Hebrews 9:28)*.

3. **Reconciled sinful humanity back to God**. Only Jesus Christ, who was both God and man, could reconcile us back to God:

> *"For if, when we were enemies, **we were reconciled to God by the death of his Son**, much more, being reconciled, we shall be saved by his life" (Romans 5:10).*

> *"And, having made peace through the blood of his cross, **by him to reconcile all things unto himself**; by him, I say, whether they be things in earth, or things in heaven. And you, that were sometime alienated and enemies in your mind by wicked works, yet now hath **he reconciled In the body of his flesh through death**, to present you holy and unblameable and unreproveable in his sight" (Colossians 1:20-22).*

> *"And all things are of God, who hath reconciled us to himself by Jesus Christ...**God was in Christ, reconciling the world unto himself**" (2 Corinthians 5:18-19).*

The words "reconciled" and "reconciling" in 2 Corinthians 5:18-19 are translated from the Greek word *katallasso*. W. E. Vine, in *Vine's Expository Dictionary of NT Words,* states that *katallasso* denotes: "to change from enmity to friendship, to reconcile"[10]

As stated by the *Webster's 1913 Online Dictionary*, the word *reconcile* can be defined as: "To cause to be friendly again...to restore to friendship"[11]

> *"(5) For there is one God, and one mediator between God and men, the man Christ Jesus; (6) Who gave himself a ransom for all" (1 Timothy 2:5-6).*

The word "mediator" in 1 Timothy 2:5 comes from the Greek word *mesites*, which means "a go-between...a reconciler." In order to be a mediator between two parties, you must have the nature of both parties. Jesus Christ was both God (1 Timothy 3:16) and man (1 Timothy 2:5).

The Victory of Jesus Christ

The death, burial, and resurrection of Jesus Christ defeated the devil and powers of darkness:

> *"Who hath **delivered us from the power of darkness**, and hath translated us into the kingdom of his dear Son: In whom we have redemption through his blood, even the forgiveness of sins" (Colossians 1:13-14).*

> *"Blotting out the handwriting of ordinances that was against us, which was contrary to us, and took it out of the way, nailing it to his cross; And **having spoiled principalities and powers, he made a shew of them openly, triumphing over them in it**" (Colossians 2:14-15).*

> *"Forasmuch then as the children are partakers of flesh and blood, he also himself likewise took part of the same; that **through death he might destroy him that had the power of death**, that is, the devil; And **deliver them who through fear of death were all their lifetime subject to bondage**" (Hebrews 2:14-15).*

4 - **The Grace of God**

"(4) But God, who is rich in mercy, for his great love wherewith he loved us, (5) Even when we were dead in sins, hath quickened us together with Christ, (by grace ye are saved;) (6) And hath raised us up together, and made us sit together in heavenly places in Christ Jesus: (7) That in the ages to come he might shew the exceeding riches of his grace in his kindness toward us through Christ Jesus. (8) For by grace are ye saved through faith; and that not of yourselves: it is the gift of God: (9) Not of works, lest any man should boast. (10) For we are his workmanship, created in Christ Jesus unto good works, which God hath before ordained that we should walk in them" (Ephesians 2:4-10).

The words "For by grace are ye saved through faith" (Ephesians 2:8, KJV) are translated as "For it is by free grace (God's unmerited favor) that you are saved (delivered from judgment and made partakers of Christ's salvation) through [your] faith" (AMPCE).

God's Grace Is His Unmerited Favor

What is the grace of God? The grace of God is "God's unmerited favor" (Ephesians 2:8, AMPCE) to everyone. God's gift of salvation to each of us, through what Jesus Christ did, is something that we could never earn or deserve.

In other words, unless God had provided a spotless Lamb as an atonement for our sins, our sins could never be covered. Unless Jesus Christ had been willing to purchase our salvation, by living a sin-free life and dying the agonizing death of crucifixion for us, we could never be saved.

Jesus let us know that He was the ***only way*** for us to be saved. A good analogy is trying to get to the moon by jumping. Some of us may jump really high, but each of us falls way short of being able to reach the moon by jumping. Similarly, only God can save our soul.

God saw that He was going to manifest Himself in the flesh (1 Timothy 3:16) and that Jesus Christ would die for the sins of the world (1 John 2:2; 4:10), ***before*** the foundation of the world:

Jesus Christ was *"the Lamb slain **from the foundation of the world"** (Revelation 13:8).*

Peter wrote, *"Ye were not redeemed with corruptible things, as silver and gold...But with the precious blood of Christ, as of a lamb without blemish and without spot: Who verily was **foreordained before the foundation of the world**, but was manifest in these last times for you" (1 Peter 1:18-20).*

God's thoughts and ways are much higher than our thoughts and ways (Isaiah 55:8-9), but think about it. How do we know how much God loves us? Because of the great love that God demonstrated toward us in manifesting Himself in Jesus Christ (1 Timothy 3:16), who died for the sins of the world:

> *"For God so loved the world, that he gave his only begotten Son, that whosoever believeth in him should not perish, but have everlasting life" (John 3:16).*

> *"But God commendeth his love toward us, in that, while we were yet sinners, Christ died for us" (Romans 5:8).*

> *"Hereby perceive we the love of God, because he laid down his life for us: and we ought to lay down our lives for the brethren" (1 John 3:16).*

God's Grace Does Not Allow Us to "Continue in Sin"

The grace of God does not allow us to have a "license for" sin (Jude 4, NIV) or "continue in sin" (Romans 6:1-2):

> *"For certain men whose condemnation was written about long ago have secretly slipped in among you. They are godless men, who change the grace of our God into a license for immorality and deny Jesus Christ our only Sovereign and Lord" (Jude 4, NIV).*

> *"What shall we say then? Shall we continue in sin, that grace may abound? God forbid, How shall we, that are dead to sin, live any longer therein?" (Romans 6:1-2).*

The words "God forbid" (Romans 6:2, KJV) are translated as "Certainly not!" (NKJV).

The Grace of God and Our Faith

God could have made each of us as a robot that was programmed to only obey His every command. However, God made each of us with a free will and allows us to make decisions and choices. But in eternity, God will have those with Him that chose to love, serve, and worship Him of their own free will.

God continually reaches out to each of us. God draws us to Himself, deals with us, and speaks to us. God visits us, stands at the door of our heart and knocks. God convicts us when we sin or if we have sin in our life. God shows us, through His written Word, that He made a way for each of us to be reconciled to God when Jesus died on the cross for our sins.

God paid the price and made a way for every person to be saved. So why are few saved (Matthew 7:13-14; Luke 13:23-27)? Because not every person has faith in God in harmony with what the Bible teaches:

Jesus said, *"And why call you me Lord, Lord and do not the things which I say?" (Luke 6:46).*

"Now faith is the substance of things hoped for, the evidence of things not seen…But without faith it is impossible to please him: for he that cometh to God must believe that he is, and that he is a rewarder of them that diligently seek him" (Hebrews 11:1, 6).

"What doth it profit, my brethren, though a man say he hath faith, and have not works? Can faith save him? If a brother or sister be naked, and destitute of daily food, And one of you say unto them, Depart in peace, be ye warmed and filled; notwithstanding ye give them not those things which are needful to the body; what doth it profit? Even so faith, if it hath not works, is dead, being alone. Yea, a man may say, Thou hast faith, and I have works: shew me thy faith without thy works, and I will shew thee my faith by my works. Thou believest that there is one God; thou doest well: the devils also believe, and tremble. But wilt thou know, O vain man, that faith without works is dead? Was not Abraham our father justified by works, when he had offered Isaac his son upon the altar? Seest thou how faith wrought with his works, and by works was faith

37

made perfect? And the scripture was fulfilled which saith, Abraham believed God, and it was imputed unto him for righteousness: and he was called the Friend of God. Ye see then how that by works a man is justified, and not by faith only. Likewise also was not Rahab the harlot justified by works, when she had received the messengers, and had sent them out another way? For as the body without the spirit is dead, so faith without works is dead also" (James 2:14-26).

In James 2:14-26, the word "works" (KJV) occurs twelve times and is translated as "deeds" (NIV).

God has given every one of us the faith that we need to respond to God's call or invitation (Romans 12:3). God created each of us as a free-moral agent and He will never override our will or choice. Each of us can choose to grieve, quench, and resist the Spirit of God *or* each of us can choose to yield to, follow, and obey the Spirit of God. Someone can choose to live contrary to God's will for their life *or* they can choose to do their best to live in harmony with God's will for their life. Even though we are allowed by God to exercise our free will, the Bible is very clear that we will all someday stand before God and give an account for our words, actions, lifestyle, and choices.

A good analogy of grace and faith can be seen when someone is drowning and a life preserver is thrown out to them. The life preserver being thrown to that drowning individual is similar to "the grace of God." The individual grabbing on to the life preserver, to save themself from drowning, is similar to someone putting their faith in God to save them. Each of us can choose death by not grabbing on to the life preserver or each of us can choose life by grabbing on to the life preserver. All credit for each of us being saved belongs to our loving God that threw the life preserver out to us as we were drowning.

Another possible illustration of grace and faith can be seen in Jesus standing at the door of our heart and knocking (Revelation 3:20). Someone can choose to keep the door of their heart closed or they can open the door of their heart. "The grace of God" is Jesus standing at the door of our heart and knocking. This "knocking" can be extending an invitation to us, dealing with us in some way, convicting us of some sin, or speaking to us in some way. Our faith in God is shown by opening the door of our heart to let Jesus in *or* our lack of faith in God is shown by keeping the door of our heart closed when Jesus is knocking.

God's Grace Empowers Us to Do His Will

The grace of God is not only the unmerited (undeserved, unearned) favor of God (Ephesians 1:7, 2:8-9), but the grace of God is also God giving us the power (ability, desire) to do whatever He has called us to do. The grace of God is not only involved in making a way for us to be saved, but the grace of God is also involved in empowering or enabling us to perform His will for our life:

> *"According to the grace of God which is given unto me, as a wise masterbuilder, I have laid the foundation, and another buildeth thereon. But let every man take heed how he buildeth thereupon" (1 Corinthians 3:10).*

> *"And when James, Cephas, and John, who seemed to be pillars, perceived the grace that was given unto me, they gave to me and Barnabas the right hands of fellowship; that we should go unto the heathen, and they unto the circumcision" (Galatians 2:9).*

> *"And God is able to make all grace abound toward you; that ye, always having all sufficiency in all things, may abound to every good work" (2 Corinthians 9:8).*

> *"And he said unto me, My grace is sufficient for thee: for my strength is made perfect in weakness" (2 Corinthians 12:9).*

> *"Whereof I was made a minister, according to the gift of the grace of God given unto me by the effectual working of his power. Unto me, who am less than the least of all saints, is this grace given, that I should preach among the Gentiles the unsearchable riches of Christ" (Ephesians 3:7-8).*

> *"But unto every one of us is given grace according to the measure of the gift of Christ" (Ephesians 4:7).*

God gives us the grace (power, desire, ability) to be successful in whatever He has called us to be or do for His glory and His

Name's sake. God will never ask us to do something that He will not enable us or give us the ability to do.

Paul gave God all of the credit for anything good that he was or did. Paul said:

> *"I am the least of the apostles, that am not meet to be called an apostle, because I persecuted the church of God. But by the grace of God I am what I am: and his grace which was bestowed upon me was not in vain; but I laboured more abundantly than they all: yet not I, but the grace of God which was with me" (1 Corinthians 15:9-10).*

Paul also said, *"For in nothing am I behind the very chiefest apostles, though I be nothing" (2 Corinthians 12:11).* Paul understood that it is the Spirit of God, working in the world or in us or through us, that accomplishes the work of God on this earth.

Jesus made similar statements:

> *"The Son can do nothing of himself" (John 5:19).*

> *"I can of mine own self do nothing" (John 5:30).*

> *"I do nothing of myself" (John 8:28).*

> *"The words that I speak unto you I speak not of myself: but the Father that dwelleth in me, he doeth the works" (John 14:10).*

The grace of God will empower us (1 Corinthians 15:10) and teach us to live a godly life in this present world:

> *"For the grace of God that bringeth salvation hath appeared to all men, Teaching us that, denying ungodliness and worldly lusts, we should live soberly, righteously, and godly, in this present world" (Titus 2:11-12).*

The Definition of "Loving God"

Our relationship with God is a relationship of love. All love is a choice. I believe that Paul had a deep love for God and more than anything, wanted to please God first and foremost (1 Thessalonians 4:1; 2 Timothy 2:4). How did Paul demonstrate his love toward God? He strove to be a continual light to others (Romans 13:12; Ephesians 5:8). He endeavored every day to be led by the Spirit of God (Romans 8:14; Galatians 5:18). He sought God in prayer to continually perform God's will for his life (Ephesians 6:18). He tried to do whatever he could to reach others with the gospel (1 Corinthians 9:19-22). He did his best to yield himself to God (Romans 6:13) and to submit his human will to God's will (1 Corinthians 15:31).

The Bible definition of "loving God" is not only feelings of love toward God, but it goes further and includes loving others and obeying God's commandments.

Jesus said:

> *"A new commandment I give unto you, That ye love one another; as I have loved you, that ye also love one another. By this shall all men know that ye are my disciples, if ye have love one to another" (John 13:34-35).*

> *"If ye love me, keep my commandments" (John 14:15).*

> *"He that hath my commandments, and keepeth them, he it is that loveth me" (John 14:21).*

> *"If a man love me, he will keep my words" (John 14:23).*

> *"This is my commandment, That ye love one another, as I have loved you. Greater love hath no man than this, that a man lay down his life for his friends. Ye are my friends, if ye do whatsoever I command you" (John 15:12-14).*

Paul wrote:

> *"Put on therefore, as the elect of God, holy and beloved, bowels of mercies, kindness, humbleness of mind, meekness, longsuffering; Forbearing one another, and forgiving one another, if any man have a quarrel against any: even as Christ forgave you, so also do ye. And above all these things put on charity, which is the bond of perfectness" (Colossians 3:12-14).*

The word "charity" (Colossians 3:14, KJV) is translated as "love" (NKJV).

Peter wrote:

> *"And above all things have fervent charity among yourselves: for charity shall cover the multitude of sins" (1 Peter 4:8).*

The word "charity" (1 Peter 4:8, KJV) is translated as "love" (NKJV).

John wrote:

> *"We love him, because he first loved us. If a man say, I love God, and hateth his brother, he is a liar: for he that loveth not his brother whom he hath seen, how can he love God whom he hath not seen? And this commandment have we from him, That he who loveth God love his brother also"* (1 John 4:19-21).

> *"Whosoever believeth that Jesus is the Christ is born of God: and every one that loveth him that begat loveth him also that is begotten of him. By this we know that we love the children of God, when we love God, and keep his commandments. For this is the love of God, that we keep his commandments: and his commandments are not grievous" (1 John 5:1-3).*

The Ultimate Goal of the Grace of God

What must we do to be saved? What must we do to have our name written in the Lamb's book of life and escape the second death, which is the lake of fire (the final destination of those that die lost)? The Bible is very clear that Jesus taught His disciples and gave them the plan of salvation to preach to the lost so that they could be saved:

> *"How shall we escape, if we neglect so great salvation; which at the first began to be spoken by the Lord, and was confirmed unto us by them that heard him" (Hebrews 2:3).*

The ultimate goal of the grace of God is for each of us to be saved (John 3:17). The grace of God made a way for every individual to be reconciled to God when they obey what the apostles preached in the book of Acts. The book of Hebrews says that Jesus is *"the author of eternal salvation unto all them that obey him" (Hebrews 5:9)*.

Jesus shed his blood for the sins of the world (1 John 2:2). God is *"not willing that any should perish, but that all should come to repentance" (2 Peter 3:9)*. It is God's will that everyone be saved and come unto the knowledge of the truth (1 Timothy 2:4), but God created man as a free-moral agent. God gives each of us a will and He allows each of us to exercise our will.

5 - <u>What Did Jesus Command His Apostles to Preach and Teach?</u>

<u>Everyone Must Be Born Again</u>

"(1) There was a man of the Pharisees, named Nicodemus, a ruler of the Jews: (2) The same came to Jesus by night, and said unto him, Rabbi, we know that thou art a teacher come from God: for no man can do these miracles that thou doest, except God be with him. (3) Jesus answered and said unto him, Verily, verily, I say unto thee, Except a man be born again, he cannot see the kingdom of God. (4) Nicodemus saith unto him, How can a man be born when he is old? Can he enter the second time into his mother's womb, and be born? (5) Jesus answered, Verily, verily, I say unto thee, Except a man be born of water and of the Spirit, he cannot enter into the kingdom of God. (6) That which is born of the flesh is flesh; and that which is born of the Spirit is spirit. (7) Marvel not that I said unto thee, Ye must be born again. (8) The wind bloweth where it listeth, and thou hearest the sound thereof, but canst not tell whence it cometh, and whither it goeth: so is every one that is born of the Spirit...(16) For God so loved the world, that he gave his only begotten Son, that whosoever believeth in him should not perish, but have everlasting life" (John 3:1-8, 16).

Verses 3-7: You must be "born again" (John 3:3, KJV) or "born again (anew, from above)" (John 3:3, AMPCE), to "see the kingdom of God." Unless you are "born of water and of the Spirit" (John 3:5) you cannot enter into the kingdom of God or become a member of God's New Testament Church (Acts 1:3; 8:12; 14:22). "Born of water" refers to when you are baptized in water. "Born of the Spirit" refers to when you receive the gift of the Holy Ghost.

Verse 8: You will "hear a sound" every time someone is "born of the Spirit" (receives the gift of the Holy Ghost).

Verse 16: According to Jesus, if we believe on Him, as the Scripture has said, we will receive the gift of the Holy Ghost (John 7:37-39). People that *"believed on the Lord Jesus Christ" (Acts 11:17)* received the gift of the Holy Ghost (Acts 10:44-48).

The Gift of the Holy Ghost

Jesus said, *"(37) If any man thirst, let him come unto me, and drink. (38) He that believeth on me, as the scripture hath said, out of his belly shall flow rivers of living water. (39) (But this spake he of the Spirit, which they that believe on him should receive: for the Holy Ghost was not yet given; because that Jesus was not yet glorified.)" (John 7:37-39).*

Verse 38: Believing in Jesus, as the Scripture has said, will include receiving the gift of the Holy Ghost. When someone receives the Holy Ghost, rivers of living water will flow out of their belly. The word "belly" (KJV) can be translated as "heart" (NKJV) or "innermost being" (AMPCE). God is the *"fountain of living waters" (Jeremiah 2:13)*. Jesus said *"out of the abundance of the heart the mouth speaketh" (Matthew 12:34)*.

Verse 39: No one received the gift of the Holy Ghost until *after* Jesus was glorified. This was *after* Jesus died, rose from the dead, and ascended into heaven (Acts 1:9-11).

Jesus said:

> *"If ye then, being evil, know how to give good gifts unto your children: how much more shall your heavenly Father give the Holy Spirit to them that ask him?" (Luke 11:13).*

> *"(16) And I will pray the Father, and he shall give you another Comforter, that he may abide with you for ever; (17) Even the Spirit of truth; whom the world cannot receive, because it seeth him not, neither knoweth him: but ye know him; for he dwelleth with you, and shall be in you. (18) I will not leave you comfortless: I will come to you" (John 14:16-18).*

> *"But the Comforter, which is the Holy Ghost, whom the Father will send in my name, he shall teach you all things, and bring all things to your remembrance, whatsoever I have said unto you" (John 14:26).*

> *"But when the Comforter is come, whom I will send unto you from the Father, even the Spirit of truth, which proceedeth from the Father, he shall testify of me" (John 15:26).*

"It is expedient for you that I go away: for if I go not away, the Comforter will not come unto you; but if I depart, I will send him unto you" (John 16:7).

Jesus told His disciples that He was *with them*, but that He would be *in them* (John 14:17). Another word for the Holy Ghost is the Comforter. The word "Comforter" (John 14:16, 26; 15:26; 16:7, KJV) is translated as "Helper" (NKJV).

The Great Commission

Jesus Christ died (Matthew 27:50), was buried in a borrowed tomb (Matthew 27:57-60), rose from the dead the third day, and appeared to many of His disciples (Matthew 28:1-10; Mark 16:1-13; Luke 24:1-11; John 20:1-18).

Jesus *"shewed himself alive after his passion by many infallible proofs, being seen of them forty days, and speaking of the things pertaining to the kingdom of God" (Acts 1:3).* During this time, Jesus gave the Great Commission to His disciples (Matthew 28:16-20; Mark 16:14-20; Luke 24:44-49). Jesus said:

"Go ye therefore, and teach all nations, baptizing them in the name of the Father, and of the Son, and of the Holy Ghost: teaching them to observe all things whatsoever I have commanded you: and lo, I am with you always, even unto the end of the world" (Matthew 28:19-20).

"Go ye into all the world, and preach the gospel to every creature. He that believeth and is baptized shall be saved; but that believeth not shall be damned. And these signs shall follow them that believe...they shall speak with new tongues" (Mark 16:15-17).

"Thus it is written, and thus it behoved Christ to suffer, and to rise from the dead the third day: and that repentance and remission of sins should be preached in his name among all nations, beginning at Jerusalem" (Luke 24:46-47).

Jesus *"commanded them that they should not depart from Jerusalem, but wait for the promise of the Father, which, saith he, ye have heard of me. For John truly baptized with water; but ye shall be baptized with the Holy Ghost not many days hence" (Acts 1:4-5).*

Jesus said: *"I send the promise of my Father upon you: but tarry ye in the city of Jerusalem, until ye be endued with power from on high" (Luke 24:49)*, and *"Ye shall receive power, after that the Holy Ghost is come upon you: and ye shall be witnesses unto me both in Jerusalem, and in all Judaea, and in Samaria, and unto the uttermost part of the earth" (Acts 1:8)*.

Our Power to Speak

What is one of the most powerful members in our body? Our tongue, when we speak. Death and life are in the power of the tongue (Proverbs 18:21). How did God create the world and everything in it? He *spoke* everything into existence (Psalm 33:6, 9). The creation account in the book of Genesis states *"and God said" (Genesis 1:3, 6, 9, 11, 14, 20, 24, 26)*.

What did Jesus do when he was tempted of the devil? He spoke the Word of God to the devil: *"It is written..." (Matthew 4:4, 7, 10)*. How did Jesus take authority over demons (Mark 9:25), storms (Mark 4:35-41), or sicknesses (Matthew 8:1-13)? He *spoke* to them. How did Jesus raise people from the dead? He *spoke* to those people (Mark 5:41; John 11:43).

How are miracles performed? By *speaking* in faith to whatever the need is in the name of Jesus (Acts 3:6; 4:10). How are demons cast out? By *speaking* to them in the name of Jesus Christ (Acts 16:18). God *"is able to do exceeding abundantly above all that we ask* [through our tongue, speech] *or think, according to the power that worketh in us" (Ephesians 3:20)*.

How are we supposed to remove "mountains" or seemingly impossible barriers or situations in our life? We are to *speak* to them (Matthew 17:20-21; 21:21-22). We know that all of our requests are subject to the will of God for our lives. John wrote, *"And this is the confidence that we have in him, that, if we ask any thing according to his will, he heareth us" (1 John 5:14)*. God can (a) make the problem smaller in our life, so that we can deal with it or (b) leave the problem the same size, but make us big enough to deal with it.

How has God ordained to spread His New Testament plan of salvation on this earth? Through the preaching and teaching of God's Word (Matthew 28:19-20; Mark 16:15, 20; Luke 24:47).

6 - <u>The Birth of God's Church</u>

<u>The Baptism of the Holy Ghost</u>

All four Gospels record that Jesus would baptize believers with the Holy Ghost (Matthew 3:11; Mark 1:8; Luke 3:16; John 1:33). John the Baptist said:

> *"I indeed baptize you with water unto repentance: but he that cometh after me is mightier than I, whose shoes I am not worthy to bear: he shall baptize you with the Holy Ghost, and with fire" (Matthew 3:11).*

Jesus Christ came to this earth to both *cleanse us* from our sins, and *fill us* with His Spirit. Jesus said:

> *"I am come that they might have life, and that they might have it more abundantly" (John 10:10).*

Jesus Christ was tempted in all points like as we are (lust of the flesh, lust of the eyes, pride of life; 1 John 2:16; Genesis 3:6; Matthew 4:1-11), *"yet without sin" (Hebrews 4:15).* Why? So that after we receive that same Spirit that dwelt in Jesus, we will have power to overcome any temptation in our life. Jesus Christ made a greater experience available to us in the New Testament:

> John wrote, *"Ye are of God, little children, and have overcome them: because greater is he that is in you, than he that is in the world" (1 John 4:4).*

> Paul wrote, *"I can do all things through Christ which strengtheneth me" (Philippians 4:13).*

In the Old Testament, the temple of God was in Jerusalem. During His earthly ministry, Jesus Christ said his body was the temple of God (John 2:19-22; 14:10). After each of us receives the gift of the Holy Ghost, our body is considered to be the temple of God (1 Corinthians 3:16-17; 6:19-20; 2 Corinthians 6:16).

In the Old Testament, the Spirit of God moved upon people and temporarily came upon people, but never took up a permanent residence in any person. In the New Testament, God takes up a permanent residence in our inner man when we are baptized with

47

His Spirit. Jesus commanded His apostles to remain in Jerusalem until they were baptized with the Holy Ghost (Acts 1:3-5). Jesus told his disciples that they *would be "endued with power from on high" (Luke 24:49)* or *"receive power" (Acts 1:8) after* they were *"baptized with the Holy Ghost" (Acts 1:5).* Jesus then ascended up into heaven from the Mount of Olives just east of Jerusalem (Acts 1:9-12; Luke 24:50-51). No one was baptized with the Holy Ghost prior to the day of Pentecost in the book of Acts chapter 2.

According to Acts 1:12-15, the following people were included in the 120 disciples at Jerusalem that were *waiting* for the promised gift of the Holy Ghost (Acts 1:4; Luke 24:49, 52-53):

- The eleven remaining apostles of Jesus.
- The women, possibly including Mary Magdalene, Mary the mother of James, Salome, and Joanna.
- Mary, the mother of Jesus.
- Jesus' half-brothers James, Joses, Simon, and Judas (sons of Joseph & Mary, the mother of Jesus; Matthew 13:55).

According to Acts 1:16-26, Matthias was appointed as one of the *"twelve apostles of the Lamb" (Revelation 21:14)* to replace Judas Iscariot, who had betrayed Jesus and then hanged himself (Matthew 27:3-10).

The Initial Outpouring of the Holy Ghost

"(1) And when the day of Pentecost was fully come, they were all with one accord in one place. (2) And suddenly there came a sound from heaven as of a rushing mighty wind, and it filled all the house where they were sitting. (3) And there appeared unto them cloven tongues like as of fire, and it sat upon each of them. (4) And they were all filled with the Holy Ghost, and began to speak with other tongues, as the Spirit gave them utterance. (5) And there were dwelling at Jerusalem Jews, devout men, out of every nation under heaven. (6) Now when this was noised abroad, the multitude came together, and were confounded, because that every man heard them speak in his own language. (7) And they were all amazed and marvelled, saying one to another, Behold, are not all these which speak Galilaeans? (8) And how hear we every man in our own tongue, wherein we were born? (9) Parthians, and Medes, and Elamites, and the dwellers in Mesopotamia, and in Judaea,

and Cappadocia, in Pontus, and Asia, (10) Phrygia, and Pamphylia, in Egypt, and in the parts of Libya about Cyrene, and strangers of Rome, Jews and proselytes, (11) Cretes and Arabians, we do hear them speak in our tongues the wonderful works of God. (12) And they were all amazed, and were in doubt, saying one to another, What meaneth this? (13) Others mocking said, These men are full of new wine. (14) But Peter, standing up with the eleven, lifted up his voice, and said unto them, Ye men of Judaea, and all ye that dwell at Jerusalem, be this known unto you, and hearken to my words: (15) For these are not drunken, as ye suppose, seeing it is but the third hour of the day. (16) But this is that which was spoken by the prophet Joel; (17) And it shall come to pass in the last days, saith God, I will pour out of my Spirit upon all flesh: and your sons and your daughters shall prophesy, and your young men shall see visions, and your old men shall dream dreams: (18) And on my servants and on my handmaidens I will pour out in those days of my Spirit; and they shall prophesy: (19) And I will shew wonders in heaven above, and signs in the earth beneath; blood, and fire, and vapour of smoke: (20) The sun shall be turned into darkness, and the moon into blood, before that great and notable day of the Lord come: (21) And it shall come to pass, that whosoever shall call on the name of the Lord shall be saved" (Acts 2:1-21).

Verse 1: The birth of God's New Testament Church occurred on the day of Pentecost. All Jewish males were required to go annually to the three main Jewish feasts of Unleavened Bread, Weeks, and Tabernacles (Exodus 23:14-17; Deuteronomy 16:16).

The Feast of Passover was a day before the Feast of Unleavened Bread (Leviticus 23:5-6; Luke 22:1). The Feast of Passover commemorated: (a) The tenth plague, which was the death of every first-born male, both men and animals in Egypt, and (b) The exodus of Israelites from Egypt on the fourteenth day of the first month Abib (Leviticus 23:5; Deuteronomy 16:1) or Nisan (Esther 3:7). God "passed over" and spared those Israelites that applied the blood of a spotless male lamb to the doorposts of their houses (Exodus 12:1-30). In the New Testament, Jesus Christ died for us as "our Passover" (1 Corinthians 5:7, NKJV).

The Feast of Weeks (Exodus 34:22; Deuteronomy 16:10, 16), which was also referred to as the Feast of Harvest (Exodus 23:16) or the Feast of Pentecost, occurred 50 days after the Feast of Passover (Leviticus 23:16). The annual Jewish Feast of Pentecost celebrated the firstfruits of the wheat harvest (Exodus 34:22), and the Ten Commandments or law given by God to Moses on Mount Sinai (Exodus chapters 19 to 20; 24:12-18; 31:18; 32:15-16). As stated in *The Adam Clarke Commentary* on "Exodus 23:14":

> The feast of PENTECOST…was celebrated fifty days after the Passover to commemorate the giving of the law on Mount Sinai, which took place fifty days after, and hence, called by the Greeks Pentecost.[12]

The Ten Commandments or law that Moses received on Mount Sinai were written by God in tables of stone (Exodus 34:1-4, 28-29). The new and better covenant (Hebrews 8:6, 8, 13; 12:24) is written by God in our hearts and minds. God said:

> *"I will make a new covenant… I will put my laws into their mind, and write them in their hearts: and I will be to them a God, and they shall be to me a people" (Hebrews 8:8-10).*

> *"I will put my laws into their hearts, and in their minds will I write them" (Hebrews 10:16).*

> *"I will make a new covenant…I will put my law in their inward parts, and write it in their hearts; and will be their God, and they shall be my people" (Jeremiah 31:31-33).*

Paul wrote, *"Ye are manifestly declared to be the epistle of Christ ministered by us, written not with ink, but with the Spirit of the living God; not in tables of stone, but in fleshy tables of the heart" (2 Corinthians 3:3).* The words "in fleshy tables of the heart" (2 Corinthians 3:3, KJV) are translated as "on tablets of flesh, that is, of the heart" (NKJV).

Verses 2-3: There were two external signs before these 120 people were filled with the Holy Ghost. These signs were:
1. They *heard* a sound from heaven as a rushing mighty wind (Acts 2:2).

2. They *saw* "cloven" (KJV) or "divided" (NKJV) tongues, as of fire, that sat upon each of them (Acts 2:3).

This is similar to what happened when they received the Ten Commandments on Mount Sinai (Exodus chapters 19 to 20; Deuteronomy chapter 5). There were some external signs (Exodus 19:16, 18; 20:18, 22; Deuteronomy 5:22-26):

1. They *heard* thunders, a very loud trumpet, and God speaking to them out of the midst of the fire.
2. They *saw* lightnings, God descending on the mountain in fire, the whole mountain shaking violently, and the smoke of the fiery mountain ascending upward.

Verse 4: They were all filled with the Holy Ghost and began to speak with other "tongues" (KJV) or "languages (tongues)" (AMPCE), as the Spirit of God "gave them utterance" (KJV) or "enabled them" (NIV).

Verses 5-13: Devout Jews from at least fifteen different countries *heard* those filled with the Holy Ghost speaking in their own tongue (language) the wonderful works of God (Acts 2:5-11). This means that more than just the twelve apostles received the baptism of the Holy Ghost. Other men and women, including Mary (the mother of Jesus), also needed to receive the glorious gift of the Holy Ghost. These devout Jews were:

1. "Confounded" (Acts 2:6, KJV) or "confused" (NKJV).
2. "Amazed" (Acts 2:7, 12).
3. "In doubt" (Acts 2:12, KJV) or "perplexed" (NKJV).

Some were saying to each other "What meaneth this?" (Acts 2:12, KJV) or "Whatever could this mean?" (NKJV). Others mocking, thinking they were drunk, said that they are "full of new wine" (Acts 2:13).

Verses 14-16: Peter stood up with the eleven apostles, "lifted up his voice," and began explaining to these Jews what they had just observed (Acts 2:14). In Acts 2:15, Peter said that those who had just been filled with the Holy Ghost were "not drunk" like they thought, because it was only the "third hour of the day" (9:00 AM). Peter said that this was the fulfillment of a prophecy spoken by the Old Testament prophet Joel (Acts 2:16).

Verses 17-21: Peter quotes Joel 2:28-32 in Acts 2:17-21 to explain what happened to the 120 disciples (Acts 1:15) that had just been filled with the Holy Ghost. Peter said that God (Acts 2:17) will pour out His Spirit upon:

1. *All* "flesh" (Acts 2:17, KJV) or "people" (NIV). This refers to *anyone* in the world, including both Jews and Gentiles.
2. Men (sons, menservants). The word "servants" (Acts 2:18, KJV) is translated as "menservants" (NKJV).
3. Women (daughters, maidservants). The word "handmaidens" (Acts 2:18, KJV) is translated as "maidservants" (NKJV).

Peter said in his message to various Jews on the Day of Pentecost, *"Therefore being by the right hand of God exalted, and having received of the Father the promise of the Holy Ghost, he hath shed forth this, which ye now see and hear" (Acts 2:33).*

Peter said that people could both *see* and *hear* when someone receives the promise of the Holy Ghost. When they were filled with the Holy Ghost, they *saw* and *heard* them speak in other tongues (languages) as the Spirit of God gave them utterance.

"A sound from heaven as of a rushing mighty wind" (Acts 2:2) and "divided tongues, as of fire" (Acts 2:3, NKJV) were only mentioned during the initial outpouring the Holy Ghost (Acts 2:1-13). However, the initial evidence of speaking in other tongues, when someone was filled with the Holy Ghost, occurs throughout the book of Acts (Acts 2:1-13; 33; 10:44-47; 19:6).

Other Prophecies for the Baptism of the Holy Ghost

Besides Joel 2:28-32, there are several other prophecies in the Old Testament for the New Testament experience of "the baptism of the Holy Ghost."

God said:

> *"And I will give them one heart, and I will put a new spirit within you; and I will take the stony heart out of their flesh, and will give them an heart of flesh: That they may walk in my statutes, and keep mine ordinances, and do them: and they shall be my people, and I will be their God"*
> *(Ezekiel 11:19-20).*

"A new heart also will I give you, and a new spirit will I put within you: and I will take away the stony heart out of your flesh, and I will give you an heart of flesh. And I will put my spirit within you, and cause you to walk in my statutes, and ye shall keep my judgments, and do them" (Ezekiel 36:26-27).

Why will God give us a new heart and His Spirit? So that we have a heart after God and are empowered to do His will.

The prophet Isaiah wrote:

"For with stammering lips and another tongue will he speak to this people. To whom he said, This is the rest wherewith ye may cause the weary to rest; and this is the refreshing: yet they would not hear" (Isaiah 28:11-12).

Under the covenant that God made with Moses and the nation of Israel (Exodus 34:27-29), the sabbath was one day of each seven-day week. The sabbath was to be a day of rest and refreshing (Exodus 20:8-11; 31:14-16):

"It is a sign between me and the children of Israel for ever: for in six days the LORD made heaven and earth, and on the seventh day he rested, and was refreshed" (Exodus 31:17).

Under the new and better covenant, of which Jesus is the mediator (Hebrews 8:6; 9:15; 12:24), the gift of the Holy Ghost has been made available to everyone of us. When we receive the Holy Ghost, it is a rest and refreshing twenty-four hours a day and seven days a week for our inner man. Jesus said:

"Come unto me, all ye that labour and are heavy laden, and I will give you rest. Take my yoke upon you, and learn of me; for I am meek and lowly in heart: and ye shall find rest unto your souls. For my yoke is easy, and my burden is light" (Matthew 11:28-30).

7 - <u>What Did the Apostles Preach and Teach?</u>

<u>Peter Preaches the Gospel</u>

On the day of Pentecost in Jerusalem, 120 people received the gift of the Holy Ghost (Acts 2:1-13). Following this, Peter preached about (a) God's gift of the Holy Ghost that some had just experienced and others had observed (Acts 2:14-21, 33), and (b) The ministry, death, and resurrection of Jesus Christ (Acts 2:22-35). Then Peter preached:

> *"(36) Therefore let all the house of Israel know assuredly, that God hath made that same Jesus, whom ye have crucified, both Lord and Christ. (37) Now when they heard this, they were pricked in their heart, and said unto Peter and to the rest of the apostles, Men and brethren, what shall we do? (38) Then Peter said unto them, Repent, and be baptized every one of you in the name of Jesus Christ for the remission of sins, and ye shall receive the gift of the Holy Ghost. (39) For the promise is unto you, and to your children, and to all that are afar off, even as many as the Lord our God shall call. (40) And with many other words did he testify and exhort, saying, Save yourselves from this untoward generation. (41) Then they that gladly received his word were baptized: and the same day there were added unto them about three thousand souls" (Acts 2:36-41).*

These people were "pricked in their heart" (Acts 2:37, KJV) or "cut to the heart" (NKJV) and asked, *"What shall we do?" (Acts 2:37).* Jesus had given Peter "the keys of the kingdom of heaven" (Matthew 16:16-19). *Peter declared the New Testament plan of salvation in Acts 2:38.* In Acts 2:38, the words "for the remission of sins" (KJV) are translated as "for the forgiveness of your sins" (NIV). God has promised to give the Holy Ghost to those that will repent of their sins and be baptized in the name of Jesus Christ. 3000 people "were baptized" (Acts 2:41), which may have included both being baptized in water in the name of Jesus Christ (Acts 2:38), and being "baptized with the Holy Ghost" (Acts 1:5).

The New Testament Plan of Salvation

The New Testament gospel is that Jesus Christ died for our sins, was buried, and rose again the third day (1 Corinthians 15:1-4). On the day of Pentecost, Peter preached about the death and resurrection of Jesus Christ *and* that to "be saved" (Mark 16:16), each of us must experience our own:

1. Death to our sins (repentance)
2. Burial (water baptism)
3. Resurrection (gift of the Holy Ghost)

Just like the Israelites had to *apply* the blood of the Passover lamb to the doors of their houses to escape death (Exodus 12:12-13; 21-30), we have to properly *apply* the blood of Christ our Passover (1 Corinthians 5:7) to our lives to be saved. For example, the blood of Jesus cleanses us when we confess our sins to God (1 John 1:7-9), washes away our sins when we are baptized in water in the name of Jesus (Acts 22:16; Revelation 1:5), and sanctifies us (Hebrews 13:12) or helps us to live a "holy" life (1 Peter 1:16) when we are filled with His Spirit (Romans 8:13). The blood of Jesus enables us to be an overcomer (Revelation 12:11).

Jesus Christ is the mediator of a new and better covenant (Hebrews 8:6; 9:15-16; 12:24), which includes our New Testament salvation. Jesus Christ *"became the author of eternal salvation unto all them that obey him" (Hebrews 5:9).* How do we obey Jesus? We obey Jesus by obeying everything that He said, which includes obeying what the apostles preached in the book of Acts.

Jesus commanded His apostles to preach:	The apostles preached:
repentance (Luke 24:47).	repentance (Acts 2:38; 3:19; 5:31; 17:30; 20:21; 26:20).
water baptism (Matthew 28:19; Mark 16:16; John 3:5).	water baptism (Acts 2:38; 2:41; 8:16; 9:18; 10:47-48; 16:14-15; 30-34; 18:8; 19:5; 22:16).
receiving the gift of the Holy Ghost (Luke 24:49; John 3:5-8; 7:37-39; Acts 1:4-5, 8).	receiving the gift of the Holy Ghost (Acts 2:38-39; 5:32; 8:14-17; 9:17; 10:44-47; 11:15-17; 15:8-9; 19:2-7).

Peter's Conversion

The Bible does not record who baptized Peter, or any of the other eleven apostles of the Lamb, in the name of Jesus for the remission of their sins. Perhaps they baptized each other in water prior to the day of Pentecost. For how could Peter and the other apostles tell others to do something that they had not yet done?

Jesus did not consider Peter "converted" until *after* he received the Holy Ghost. The night before Jesus' death, Jesus told Peter, who was also called Simon (Matthew 10:2; 16:16-17; Luke 6:14):

> *"Simon, Simon, behold, Satan hath desired to have you, that he may sift you as wheat: But I have prayed for thee, that thy faith fail not: and when thou art converted, strengthen thy brethren" (Luke 22:31-32).*

Then Jesus told Peter that he would deny knowing Him three times before the rooster crowed (Matthew 26:34; Mark 14:30; Luke 22:34; John 13:38). While Jesus was bound and being examined by the Jewish high priest and Sanhedrin, Peter denied that he knew Jesus three times. Immediately following Peter's third denial, the rooster crowed, Jesus turned and looked upon Peter, and Peter went out and wept bitterly (Matthew 26:75; Mark 14:72; Luke 22:60-62; John 18:27). Peter truly loved Jesus and was very sorry that he had denied Him three times. After Peter received the gift of the Holy Ghost (Acts 2:1-4), we never read about him denying Jesus. Instead, we read about Peter being "filled with the Holy Ghost" and speaking the word of God with boldness (Acts 4:8, 13, 31).

Peter's Other Gospel Messages

God worked through Peter to heal a lame man asking alms at the Beautiful gate of the temple in Jerusalem (Acts 3:1-11). After this lame man was miraculously healed, Peter preached to the people near the temple about the death and resurrection of Jesus (Acts 3:12-18) and then said:

> *"(19) Repent ye therefore, and be converted, that your sins may be blotted out, when the times of refreshing shall come from the presence of the Lord; (20) And he shall send Jesus Christ, which before was preached unto you" (Acts 3:19-20).*

57

The apostles Peter and John were put in "jail" (Acts 4:3, NIV) by the Jewish leaders in Jerusalem who were *"grieved that they taught the people, and preached through Jesus the resurrection from the dead" (Acts 4:2)*. *"Howbeit many of them which heard the word believed; and the number of the men was about five thousand" (Acts 4:4)*. The next day, when Peter and John appeared before the Jewish "Sanhedrin" (Acts 4:15, NIV), they were asked, *"By what power, or by what name, have ye done this?" (Acts 4:7)*.

"(8) Then Peter, filled with the Holy Ghost, said unto them, Ye rulers of the people, and elders of Israel, (9) If we this day be examined of the good deed done to the impotent man, by what means he is made whole; (10) Be it known unto you all, and to all the people of Israel, that by the name of Jesus Christ of Nazareth, whom ye crucified, whom God raised from the dead, even by him doth this man stand here before you whole. (11) This is the stone which was set at nought of you builders, which is become the head of the corner. (12) Neither is there salvation in any other: for there is none other name under heaven given among men, whereby we must be saved" (Acts 4:8-12).

In Jerusalem, God worked through his apostles to perform many signs, wonders, and healings (Acts 5:12-16). There was significant church growth (Acts 5:14) and the apostles were put in the "common prison" (Acts 5:18, KJV) or "public jail" (NIV) by the Jewish high priest and his supporters. *"But the angel of the Lord by night opened the prison doors, and brought them forth, and said, Go, stand and speak in the temple to the people all the words of this life" (Acts 5:19-20)*. "All the words of this life" (Acts 5:20, KJV) are translated as "the full message of this new life" (NIV). Peter and the other apostles, who were teaching people in the temple, were again brought before the Jewish "Sanhedrin" (Acts 5:27, NIV). *"The high priest asked them, Saying, Did not we straitly command you that ye should not teach in this name? and, behold, ye have filled Jerusalem with your doctrine, and intend to bring this man's blood upon us" (Acts 5:27-28)*.

"(29) Then Peter and the other apostles answered and said, We ought to obey God rather than men. (30) The God of our

58

fathers raised up Jesus, whom ye slew and hanged on a tree. (31) Him hath God exalted with his right hand to be a Prince and a Saviour, for to give repentance to Israel, and forgiveness of sins. (32) And we are his witnesses of these things; and so is also the Holy Ghost, whom God hath given to them that obey him" (Acts 5:29-32).

Peter's messages to others about Jesus Christ (Acts 3:12-18; 4:10; 5:30-32) and their proper response (Acts 3:19-20; 4:12; 5:31-32) were not as detailed as his first message (Acts 2:14-40). However, Peter certainly did not change his Acts 2:38 message of salvation.

When Peter preached the gospel (Acts 15:7), it always included the death and resurrection of Jesus Christ (Acts 10:36-43) *and* that to "be saved" (Acts 11:14), each of us must experience our own:

1.   Death to our sins (repentance; Acts 11:18).
2.   Burial (water baptism; Acts 10:47-48).
3.   Resurrection (gift of the Holy Ghost; Acts 10:44-47; 11:15-17; 15:8).

Peter also stated that through the grace of God and our faith (Acts 10:43, 11:17, 15:7-9, 11), *"we shall be saved" (Acts 15:11).*

Paul's Gospel Message

Paul preached the same Acts 2:38 message of salvation as Peter. Paul preached about:

1.   **Repentance**. Paul said, *"God...commandeth all men every where to repent" (Acts 17:30).* Paul testified, *"both to the Jews, and also to the Greeks, repentance toward God, and faith toward our Lord Jesus Christ" (Acts 20:21).*

2.   **Water baptism**. Paul baptized people in water *"in the name of the Lord Jesus" (Acts 19:5).*

3.   **The gift of the Holy Ghost**. Paul asked others *"Did you receive the Holy Spirit when you believed?" (Acts 19:2; NKJV).* These individuals told Paul that they had not yet received the Holy Ghost (Acts 19:2). After Paul baptized these people, he laid his hands on them and they received the Holy Ghost with the initial evidence of speaking in tongues (Acts 19:6-7).

Chronology of Book of Acts & Life of Paul

Date A.D.	Chronology of Book of Acts & Life of Paul
30	Ascension of Christ; Birth of the Church (Acts 1:1-2:47)
around 33	Conversion of Paul (Acts 9:1-19)
44	Death of Herod Agrippa I (Acts 12:23)
47-48	Paul's First Missionary Journey (Acts 13:1-14:28)
? 48	Paul wrote GALATIANS
49	Council in Jerusalem (Acts 15:1-35)
49-52	Paul's Second Missionary Journey (Acts 15:36-18:22)
50	Paul wrote 1 & 2 THESSALONIANS
52-57	Paul's 3rd Missionary Journey (Acts 18:23-21:17)
55-56	Paul wrote 1 & 2 CORINTHIANS
early 57	Paul wrote ROMANS
May 57	Paul's arrest in Jerusalem (Acts 21:18-23:30)
57-59	Paul's appearance before Felix; imprisonment in Caesarea for two years (Acts 23:31-24:27)
59	Paul's appearances before Festus and King Herod Agrippa II (Acts 24:1-26:32)
September 59 - February 60	Paul's journey to Rome (Acts 27:1-28:14)
60-62	Paul's first Roman imprisonment under house-arrest (Acts 28:14-31)
? 60-62	Paul wrote PHILEMON, COLOSSIANS, EPHESIANS, PHILIPPIANS
?	Paul's release from first Roman imprisonment
?	Paul wrote 1 TIMOTHY, TITUS, 2 TIMOTHY
? 65	Paul's second Roman imprisonment and martyrdom under Roman emperor Nero
Epistles written by the Apostle Paul are listed in *all capital letters*. Dates are taken from the book *Paul: Apostle of the Heart Set Free* by F.F. Bruce[13, 14, 15]	

The Gospel Preached by the Apostles

Paul wrote that this New Testament salvation message is something that transforms us into a completely new creature:

> *"Therefore if any man be in Christ, he is a new creature: old things are passed away; behold, all things are become new" (2 Corinthians 5:17).*

When Peter, Paul and the other apostles preached the gospel, it included both what Jesus *did* (died for our sins, was buried, and rose again the third day) *and what we must do* for our salvation. In other words, the preaching of the gospel included *how we must respond* to the death, burial, and resurrection of Jesus Christ so that we can "be saved" (Acts 16:31).

The New Testament epistles were written to churches or individuals that had already obeyed the Acts 2:38 plan of salvation that was preached by the apostles in the book of Acts. For example, Paul wrote epistles to the Corinthians after they had already believed and were baptized:

> *"And Crispus, the chief ruler of the synagogue, believed on the Lord with all his house; and many of the Corinthians hearing believed, and were baptized" (Acts 18:8).*

Paul wrote an epistle to the church at Ephesus after they had already been baptized and received the gift of the Holy Ghost:

> Paul, *"said unto them, Unto what then were ye baptized? And they said, Unto John's baptism. Then said Paul, John verily baptized with the baptism of repentance, saying unto the people, that they should believe on him which should come after him, that is, on Christ Jesus. When they heard this, they were baptized in the name of the Lord Jesus. And when Paul had laid his hands upon them, the Holy Ghost came on them; and they spake with tongues, and prophesied. And all the men were about twelve" (Acts 19:3-7).*

These churches or individuals had become members of God's New Testament church *after* they repented of their sins, were baptized in Jesus' name for the remission of their sins, and received the gift of the Holy Ghost. We can see this more clearly if we look at some New Testament Epistles.

61

Epistle of Paul to the Romans

Paul wrote to: *"All that be in Rome, beloved of God, called to be saints" (Romans 1:7).* He had not yet been in Rome to preach the gospel (Romans 1:15-16). Paul gave them detailed explanations of the gospel of Jesus Christ (Romans 16:25-26).

1. **Repentance**:

   "Shall we continue in sin, that grace may abound? God forbid. How shall we, that are dead to sin, live any longer therein? ...our old man is crucified with him, that the body of sin might be destroyed, that henceforth we should not serve sin. For he that is dead is freed from sin" (Romans 6:1-2, 6-7).

2. **Water baptism:**

   "Know ye not, that so many of us as were baptized into Jesus Christ were baptized into his death? Therefore we are buried with him by baptism into death: that like as Christ was raised up from the dead by the glory of the Father, even so we also should walk in newness of life. For if we have been planted together in the likeness of his death, we shall be also in the likeness of his resurrection" (Romans 6:3-5).

3. **The gift of the Holy Ghost**:

   "But ye are not in the flesh, but in the Spirit, if so be that the Spirit of God dwell in you. Now if any man have not the Spirit of Christ, he is none of his. And if Christ be in you, the body is dead because of sin; but the Spirit is life because of righteousness. But if the Spirit of him that raised up Jesus from the dead dwell in you, he that raised up Christ from the dead shall also quicken your mortal bodies by his Spirit that dwelleth in you...For if ye live after the flesh, ye shall die: but if ye through the Spirit do mortify the deeds of the body, ye shall live. For as many as are led by the Spirit of God, they are the sons of God. For ye have not received the spirit of bondage again to fear; but ye have received the Spirit of adoption, whereby we cry, Abba, Father. The Spirit itself beareth witness with our spirit, that we are the children of God" (Romans 8:9-11, 13-16).

Epistles of Paul to the Corinthians

Paul's epistles to the Corinthians were addressed to: *"The church of God which is at Corinth, to them that are sanctified in Christ Jesus, called to be saints" (1 Corinthians 1:2)*, and *"The church of God which is at Corinth, with all the saints which are in all Achaia (2 Corinthians 1:1)*. Paul wrote further instructions on the gospel that he preached to those in Corinth (1 Corinthians 15:1-4) during his second missionary journey (Acts 18:1-18).

1. **Repentance**:

   "I die daily" (1 Corinthians 15:31).

   "Now I rejoice, not that ye were made sorry, but that ye sorrowed to repentance: for ye were made sorry after a godly manner...For godly sorrow worketh repentance to salvation" (2 Corinthians 7:9-10).

2. **Water baptism**:

   "Is Christ divided? was Paul crucified for you? or were ye baptized in the name of Paul? I thank God that I baptized none of you, but Crispus and Gaius; Lest any should say that I had baptized in mine own name. And I baptized also the household of Stephanas" (1 Corinthians 1:13-16).

   "And such were some of you: but ye are washed, but ye are sanctified, but ye are justified in the name of the Lord Jesus, and by the Spirit of our God" (1 Corinthians 6:11).

3. **The gift of the Holy Ghost**:

   "Know ye not that ye are the temple of God, and that the Spirit of God dwelleth in you?" (1 Corinthians 3:16).

   "Know ye not that your body is the temple of the Holy Ghost which is in you, which ye have of God, and ye are not your own?" (1 Corinthians 6:19).

   "For by one Spirit are we all baptized into one body, whether we be Jews or Gentiles, whether we be bond or free; and have been all made to drink into one Spirit" (1 Corinthians 12:13).

"God; Who hath also sealed us, and given the earnest of the Spirit in our hearts" (2 Corinthians 1:21-22).

"God, who also hath given unto us the earnest of the Spirit" (2 Corinthians 5:5).

"And what agreement hath the temple of God with idols? For ye are the temple of the living God; as God hath said, I will dwell in them, and walk in them; and I will be their God, and they shall be my people" (2 Corinthians 6:16).

"Examine yourselves, whether ye be in the faith; prove your own selves. Know ye not your own selves, how that Jesus Christ is in you, except ye be reprobates?" (2 Corinthians 13:5).

Epistle of Paul to the Galatians

Paul wrote to: *"The churches of Galatia" (Galatians 1:2).* Paul explained more information on the gospel that he had previously preached to them (Galatians 4:13).

1. **Repentance**:

   "I am crucified with Christ: nevertheless I live; yet not I, but Christ liveth in me: and the life which I now live in the flesh I live by the faith of the Son of God, who loved me, and gave himself for me" (Galatians 2:20).

   "And they that are Christ's have crucified the flesh with the affections and lusts" (Galatians 5:24).

   "But God forbid that I should glory, save in the cross of our Lord Jesus Christ, by whom the world is crucified unto me, and I unto the world" (Galatians 6:14).

2. **Water baptism:**

   "For ye are all the children of God by faith in Christ Jesus. For as many of you as have been baptized into Christ have put on Christ" (Galatians 3:26-27).

3. **The gift of the Holy Ghost**:

"Received ye the Spirit by the works of the law, or by the hearing of faith?" (Galatians 3:2).

"And because ye are sons, God hath sent forth the Spirit of his Son into your hearts, crying, Abba, Father" (Galatians 4:6).

"Walk in the Spirit, and ye shall not fulfil the lust of the flesh" (Galatians 5:16).

"But the fruit of the Spirit is love, joy, peace, longsuffering, gentleness, goodness, faith, Meekness, temperance" (Galatians 5:22-23).

Epistle of Paul to the Ephesians

Paul wrote to: *"The saints which are at Ephesus, and to the faithful in Christ Jesus" (Ephesians 1:1).* Paul gave more details on the gospel that he had preached to those in Ephesus (Acts 20:21; 24-25) during his third missionary journey (Acts 19:1-7).

1. **Repentance**:

"That ye put off concerning the former conversation the old man, which is corrupt according to the deceitful lusts; And be renewed in the spirit of your mind; And that ye put on the new man, which after God is created in righteousness and true holiness" (Ephesians 4:22-24).

2. **Water baptism**:

"One Lord, one faith, one baptism" (Ephesians 4:5).

3. **The gift of the Holy Ghost**:

"In whom ye also trusted, after that ye heard the word of truth, the gospel of your salvation: in whom also after that ye believed, ye were sealed with that holy Spirit of promise, Which is the earnest of our inheritance until the redemption of the purchased possession, unto the praise of his glory" (Ephesians 1:13-14).

"That he would grant you, according to the riches of his glory, to be strengthened with might by his Spirit in the inner man" (Ephesians 3:16).

"One God and Father of all, who is above all, and through all, and in you all" (Ephesians 4:6).

"And grieve not the holy Spirit of God, whereby ye are sealed unto the day of redemption" (Ephesians 4:30).

Epistle of Paul to the Colossians

Paul wrote to: *"The saints and faithful brethren in Christ which are at Colosse" (Colossians 1:2).* Paul explained more about the gospel, which they had previously heard (Colossians 1:5-6, 23).

1. **Repentance**:

   "Therefore, if you died with Christ from the basic principles of the world" (Colossians 2:20, NKJV).

   "Set your affection on things above, not on things on the earth. For ye are dead, and your life is hid with Christ in God" (Colossians 3:2-3).

   "Put off all these; anger, wrath, malice, blasphemy, filthy communication out of your mouth. Lie not one to another, seeing that ye have put off the old man with his deeds; And have put on the new man, which is renewed in knowledge after the image of him that created him" (Colossians 3:8-10).

2. **Water baptism**:

   "Christ...In whom also ye are circumcised with the circumcision made without hands, in putting off the body of the sins of the flesh by the circumcision of Christ: Buried with Him in baptism...having forgiven you all trespasses" (Colossians 2:8, 11-13).

3. **The gift of the Holy Ghost**:

   "To whom God would make known what is the riches of the glory of this mystery among the Gentiles; which is Christ in you, the hope of glory" (Colossians 1:27).

   "Wherein also ye are risen with him through the faith of the operation of God, who hath raised him from the dead. And you...hath he quickened together with him." (Colossians 2:12-13).

8 - <u>Repentance</u>

<u>God's Desire for Everyone to Repent</u>

Jesus Christ (Matthew 4:17; Mark 1:15; 2:17; Luke 5:32; 13:3; 15:7, 10), His forerunner John the Baptist (Matthew 3:1-11; Mark 1:4-5; Luke 3:2-14; Acts 13:24; 19:4), and His apostles (Mark 6:12; Luke 24:47; Acts 2:38; 3:19; 5:31; 17:30; 20:21; 26:20) preached about our need to repent.

We need to repent when we initially come to God, but we will also need to periodically repent after we become a member of God's New Testament Church. Jesus spoke to five of the seven churches in Asia Minor, while the Apostle John was still alive, about their need to repent (Revelation 2:5, 16, 21-22; 3:3, 19).

"God is love" (1 John 4:8, 16), but God hates sin:

> *"These six things doth the LORD hate: yea, seven are an abomination unto him: A proud look, a lying tongue, and hands that shed innocent blood, An heart that deviseth wicked imaginations, feet that be swift in running to mischief, A false witness that speaketh lies, and he that soweth discord among brethren" (Proverbs 6:16-19).*

> *"And let none of you imagine evil in your hearts against his neighbour; and love no false oath: for all these are things that I hate, saith the LORD" (Zechariah 8:17).*

Every action that God takes to try to restore our relationship with Him is done "in love." God has *"no pleasure in the death of the wicked" (Ezekiel 33:11)* and is *"not willing that any should perish, but that all should come to repentance" (2 Peter 3:9).* God is *"a gracious God, and merciful, slow to anger, and of great kindness" (Jonah 4:2).* God is angry with us when we sin:

> *"Take heed to yourselves, that your heart be not deceived, and ye turn aside, and serve other gods, and worship them; And then the LORD's wrath be kindled against you, and he shut up the heaven, that there be no rain, and that the land yield not her fruit; and lest ye perish quickly from off the good land which the LORD giveth you"*
> *(Deuteronomy 11:16-17).*

However, God will not continue to be angry with us, if we will repent of our sin:

> *"Return, thou backsliding Israel, saith the LORD; and I will not cause mine anger to fall upon you: for I am merciful, saith the LORD, and I will not keep anger for ever. Only acknowledge thine iniquity, that thou hast transgressed against the LORD thy God, and hast scattered thy ways to the strangers under every green tree, and ye have not obeyed my voice, saith the LORD." (Jeremiah 3:12-13).*

> *"Who is a God like unto thee, that pardoneth iniquity, and passeth by the transgression of the remnant of his heritage? He retaineth not his anger for ever, because he delighteth in mercy. He will turn again, he will have compassion upon us; he will subdue our iniquities; and thou wilt cast all their sins into the depths of the sea" (Micah 7:18-19).*

Repentance is part of God's process to restore our fellowship with Him. It is God's way of cleaning us up so that He can work through us to be a blessing to others. Our entire relationship with God is a "love" relationship. If we truly love God, we will also hate evil and strive to do good:

> *"Ye that love the LORD, hate evil" (Psalm 97:10).*

> *"Depart from evil and do good; seek peace and pursue it" (Psalm 34:14).*

> *"As we have therefore opportunity, let us do good unto all men, especially unto them who are of the household of faith" (Galatians 6:10).*

> *"Let love be without dissimulation. Abhor that which is evil; cleave to that which is good" (Romans 12:9).*

The word "dissimulation" (Romans 12:9, KJV) is translated as "hypocrisy" (NKJV).

If we turn to God, God will turn to us (Zechariah 1:3). If we draw nigh to God, God will draw nigh to us (James 4:8).

True (Genuine) Repentance

What is true (genuine) repentance? To answer this question, let us begin with an explanation of what true repentance is *not*. It is *not*:

- Just saying you are sorry
- Being sorry because you got caught
- Being sorry because of your present circumstances or problems
- Weeping and then going out and committing the same sin
- Something shallow
- Something that leaves your desires unchanged
- Just seeking a place of relief from the guilt

True repentance can be thought of as a *death* to our sin or sins:

> *"Shall we continue in sin, that grace may abound? God forbid. How shall we, that are dead to sin, live any longer therein?" (Romans 6:1-2).*

> *"Likewise reckon ye also yourselves to be dead indeed unto sin, but alive unto God through Jesus Christ our Lord" (Romans 6:11).*

> *"Who his own self bare our sins in his own body on the tree, that we, being dead to sins, should live unto righteousness" (1 Peter 2:24).*

We must admit that we have a problem and need God's help, before we will repent:

> *"They that are whole need not a physician; but they that are sick" (Luke 5:31).*

We will only seek God in repentance if we have a proper understanding of sin or sinful behavior, as shown in the Bible. This is why we need to study the Bible (2 Timothy 2:15).

True repentance includes a change (transformation) in:

1. **Our mind (thinking, intellect).** We make a conscious decision to stop any sinful behavior and give our life to God. We should strive to have the selfless "mind of Christ" (Philippians 2:1-8). This includes a change in our priorities, or what we think is important:

    "Be not conformed to this world: but be ye transformed by the renewing of your mind, that ye may prove what is that good, and acceptable, and perfect, will of God" (Romans 12:2).

    "Put off concerning the former conversation the old man, which is corrupt according to the deceitful lusts; And be renewed in the spirit of your mind" (Ephesians 4:22-23).

    "Set your affection on things above, not on things on the earth" (Colossians 3:2).

    Instead of looking at things our way, God will help us to look at things His way. It will include a different opinion, a different attitude.

2. **Our heart (emotions, feelings).** As Jesus stands at the door of our heart and knocks, we let Him in (Revelation 3:20). For it be a permanent change in our heart, we have to let God in there to touch us and change us. It is not only something that we do, but it includes something that God does in us. It is God performing surgery in our heart.

    Instead of being cold or indifferent to God, we have a love for God. Instead of wanting to flirt with sin, we hate sin. Instead of wanting to be involved in ungodly or sinful activities, we want to be involved in the work of God. Instead of just wanting to "do our own thing," we desire to pray and do our best to perform His will in our lives. Instead of desiring any temporal thing in this world, such as riches or worldly fame, we desire to put God and His cause *first* (Matthew 6:33), regardless of whatever sacrifice it may require on our part. We desire to love God with *all* of our heart, soul, strength, and mind (Luke 10:27). We desire to do whatever we can to help others "be saved" (Romans 1:14; 1 Corinthians 9:19-23).

3. **Our direction.** Instead of continuing to live a life of sin, we turn away from our sins and strive to please God:

> *"Again, when the wicked man turneth away from his wickedness that he hath committed, and doeth that which is lawful and right, he shall save his soul alive. Because he considereth, and turneth away from all his transgressions that he hath committed, he shall surely live, he shall not die. Yet saith the house of Israel, The way of the Lord is not equal. O house of Israel, are not my ways equal? Are not your ways unequal? Therefore I will judge you, O house of Israel, every One according to his ways, saith the LORD God. Repent, and turn yourselves from all your transgressions; so iniquity shall not be your ruin"*
> *(Ezekiel 18:27-30).*

Jesus said that He was going to send Paul to the Gentiles:

> *"To open their eyes, and to turn them from darkness to light, and from the power of Satan unto God, that they may receive forgiveness of sins, and inheritance among them which are sanctified by faith that is in me" (Acts 26:18).*

Paul wrote:

> *"For they themselves shew of us what manner of entering in we had unto you, and how ye turned to God from idols to serve the living and true God"*
> *(1 Thessalonians 1:9).*

We are to do our best to seek God for His direction and His will for our life. Concerning the will of God for our life: we can understand it in our mind, and feel it in our heart, but we must still take the necessary steps to actually do it. For example, we may be troubled in our mind or feel bad in our heart when we lie, cheat, or steal. However, if we continue to do these sins, then we have not yet repented or changed our behavior. When Paul reasoned to Felix of righteousness, temperance, and judgment to come, *"Felix trembled, and answered, Go thy way for this time; when I have a convenient season, I will call for thee" (Acts 24:25).* Perhaps Felix was convicted of various sins in his mind or in his heart as Paul spoke to him, but it does not mean that he repented or changed his behavior.

Genuine repentance does not mean that we "have arrived" or are perfect. However, genuine repentance includes a transformation of the way that we think, our desires, and the direction that we want to go in our life. The most important thing is the change in direction that we desire to go. Instead of wanting to live a life of sin, we want to do our best to show our love to the holy sinless God that we are striving to please. We realize how awesome the God is that we serve. The more that we find out about our glorious God, the more that we want to live for Him and do what is pleasing in His sight.

God's Role in Repentance

Without God, we *"can do nothing" (John 15:5)*. God is very involved during the process of repentance:

1. **No one can come to God (Jesus), unless God draws them.** Jesus said:

   > *"No man can come to me, except the Father which hath sent me draw him" (John 6:44).*

   > *"No man can come unto me, except it were given unto him of my Father" (John 6:65).*

   > *"And I, if I be lifted up from the earth, will draw all men unto me" (John 12:32).*

2. **The "goodness" (Romans 2:4, KJV) or "kindness" (NIV) of God leads us to repentance.** Paul wrote:

   > *"Or despisest thou the riches of his goodness and forbearance and longsuffering; not knowing that the goodness of God leadeth thee to repentance?" (Romans 2:4).*

3. **When God visits us, He will convict us of any sin in our life.**
   a. Jesus said that when the Comforter (or Holy Spirit) is come:

   > *"He will reprove the world of sin, and of righteousness, and of judgment" (John 16:8).* The word "reprove" (John 16:8, KJV) is translated as "convict" (NKJV).

   b. When Isaiah got in the presence of a holy God, he said:

   > *"Woe is me! For I am undone; because I am a man of unclean lips, and I dwell in the midst of a people of unclean*

*lips: for mine eyes have seen the King, the LORD of hosts"
(Isaiah 6:5).* The words "I am undone" (Isaiah 6:5, KJV)
are translated as "I am ruined!" (NIV).

c. After God spoke with Job and asked him numerous
    questions in Job chapters 38 to 40, Job said:

    *"Behold, I am vile, what shall I answer thee? I will lay
    mine hand upon my mouth" (Job 40:4).* The words "I am
    vile" (Job 40:4, KJV) are translated as "I am unworthy"
    (NIV).

d. After God asked Job more questions in Job chapters 40 to
    41, Job said:

    *"I have heard of thee by the hearing of the ear: but now
    mine eye seeth thee. Wherefore I abhor myself, and repent
    in dust and ashes" (Job 42:5-6).* The words "I abhor
    myself" (Job 42:6, KJV) are translated as "I despise
    myself" (NIV).

**4. As our loving Father, God will discipline and rebuke us for
our own good.**

> *"O LORD, rebuke me not in thy wrath: neither chasten me
> in thy hot displeasure. For thine arrows stick fast in me,
> and thy hand presseth me sore. There is no soundness in my
> flesh because of thine anger; neither is there any rest in my
> bones because of my sin" (Psalm 38:1-3).*

> *"Remove thy stroke away from me: I am consumed by the
> blow of thine hand. When thou with rebukes dost correct
> man for iniquity" (Psalm 39:10-11).*

> *"My son, despise not thou the chastening of the Lord, nor
> faint when thou art rebuked of him: For whom the Lord
> loveth he chasteneth, and scourgeth every son whom he
> receiveth" (Hebrews 12:5-6).*

> *"My son, do not make light of the Lord's discipline, and do
> not lose heart when he rebukes you, because the Lord
> disciplines those he loves, and he punishes everyone he
> accepts as a son" (Hebrews 12:5-6, NIV).*

Jesus said, *"As many as I love, I rebuke and chasten: be zealous therefore, and repent" (Revelation 3:19).*

The word "chasten" (Revelation 3:19, KJV) is translated as "discipline" (NIV).

5. God gives us repentance.

"Him hath God exalted with his right hand to be a Prince and a Saviour, for to give repentance to Israel, and forgiveness of sins. And we are his witnesses of these things; and so is also the Holy Ghost, whom God hath given to them that obey him" (Acts 5:31-32).

"When they heard these things, they held their peace, and glorified God, saying, Then hath God also to the Gentiles granted repentance unto life" (Acts 11:18).

"In meekness instructing those that oppose themselves; if God peradventure will give them repentance to the acknowledging of the truth" (2 Timothy 2:25).

6. Godly sorrow works (produces, brings) repentance that leads to salvation.

"(9) Now I rejoice, not that ye were made sorry, but that ye sorrowed to repentance: for ye were made sorry after a godly manner, that ye might receive damage by us in nothing. (10) For godly sorrow worketh repentance to salvation not to be repented of: but the sorrow of the world worketh death. (11) For behold this selfsame thing, that ye sorrowed after a godly sort, what carefulness it wrought in you, yea, what clearing of yourselves, yea, what indignation, yea, what fear, yea, what vehement desire, yea, what zeal, yea, what revenge! In all things ye have approved yourselves to be clear in this matter" (2 Corinthians 7:9-11).

According to 2 Corinthians 7:11, godly sorrow includes:

a. "Carefulness" (KJV) or "diligence" (NKJV) or "earnestness" (NIV). Being careful to not repeat any past sins or mistakes. Departing from evil and doing good.

b. "Clearing of yourselves" (KJV) or "eagerness to clear yourselves" (NIV). If necessary, correct any misconduct (apologize, tell the truth, pay for any property damage, return anything stolen, etc.). Change any previous improper behavior and do what is right in God's eyes.

    c. "Indignation" (KJV) or "indignation [at the sin]" (AMPCE). Having a displeasure or disgust at sin.

    d. "Fear." What are we to fear? We are to fear God (Deuteronomy 10:12; 1 Samuel 12:24). What does it mean to fear God? Under the subject "Fear," W.E. Vine states:

> The people who were delivered from Egypt saw God's great power, "feared the Lord, and believed the Lord, and his servant Moses" (Exod. 14:31). There is more involved here than mere psychological fear. The people also showed proper "honor" ("reverence") for God and "stood in awe of" Him.[16]

God puts a fear of Himself in our hearts (Jeremiah 32:39-40) and only God (Isaiah 8:13) should be the object of our fear (reverential awe). We are to show proper respect to everyone and love people, *but* we are *only* to fear God (1 Peter 2:17; Matthew 10:28; 22:39). God is in a totally different category. God, as our Creator, knows more about us than we know about ourselves (Psalm 139:1-6; Jeremiah 17:9-10; Hebrews 4:13) and He controls the air that we breath (Job 12:10; Daniel 5:23). We are to continually fear (Deuteronomy 14:23; Joshua 4:23-24; Proverbs 23:17) the loving and holy God that we will someday stand before in judgment (Matthew 10:28; 12:36-37).

    The fear of God is the beginning of knowledge (Proverbs 1:7) and wisdom (Proverbs 9:10). Wicked or evil people do not have a proper fear of God (Psalm 36:1; Proverbs 1:29; Jeremiah 2:19; Romans 3:18).

    Having a proper fear of God will cause us to hate evil (Proverbs 8:13), depart from evil (Proverbs 16:6), be obedient (Genesis 22:12), treat others fairly (Genesis 42:18), and avoid sin (Exodus 20:20).

    God takes pleasure in (Psalm 147:11), pities (Psalm 103:13), blesses (Psalm 115:13), saves (Psalm 145:19), and shows great mercy toward (Psalm 103:11) those that fear Him.

When people heard the Word of God being preached or taught, they responded differently:

"Now when they heard this, they were cut to the heart, and said to Peter and the rest of the apostles, 'Men and brethren, what shall we do?'" (Acts 2:37, NKJV).

"When they heard that, they were cut to the heart, and took counsel to slay them" (Acts 5:33).

The same sun that melts wax, hardens clay. When we are convicted by the Spirit of God, we can either yield to Him (Romans 6:13) or resist Him (Acts 7:51). We need to yield to God when He is dealing with us, since God will only give us a certain amount of time to repent of our sin (Revelation 2:21-22).

How to Repent

The following steps explain how to repent:

1. Understand and admit our sins.

a. We must understand and admit that we are a sinner in need of a Savior:

"And the publican, standing afar off, would not lift up so much as his eyes unto heaven, but smote upon his breast, saying, God be merciful to me a sinner" (Luke 18:13).

We *"...are all under sin. As it is written, There is none righteous, no, not one: There is none that understandeth, there is none that seeketh after God...that every mouth may be stopped, and all the world may become guilty before God...For all have sinned, and come short of the glory of God" (Romans 3:9-11, 19, 23).*

"Wherefore, as by one man sin entered into the world, and death by sin; and so death passed upon all men, for that all have sinned" (Romans 5:12).

b. We must understand and admit any sins that God (Job 40:4, 42:5-6; 38:1-3; 39:9-10; John 16:8; Hebrews 12:5-6; Revelation 3:19) or someone else has shown us (2 Samuel 12:1-13; Acts 2:36-37). We should be convicted and realize our guilt:

"I acknowledged my sin unto thee, and mine iniquity have I not hid. I said, I will confess my transgressions unto the LORD; and thou forgavest the iniquity of my sin"
(Psalm 32:5).

"And David said unto Nathan, I have sinned against the LORD. And Nathan said unto David, The LORD also hath put away thy sin; thou shalt not die" (2 Samuel 12:13).

c. We should ask God to search our hearts and show us any sins that we have committed; we should examine ourselves:

"Search me, O God, and know my heart: try me, and know my thoughts: And see if there be any wicked way in me, and lead me in the way everlasting" (Psalm 139:23-24).

"But let a man examine himself" (1 Corinthians 11:28).

2. Confess our sins to God.

a. We should ask God to have mercy on us and forgive us, while confessing our sins to Him:

"But if we walk in the light, as he is in the light, we have fellowship one with another, and the blood of Jesus Christ his Son cleanseth us from all sin. If we say that we have no sin, we deceive ourselves, and the truth is not in us. If we confess our sins, he is faithful and just to forgive us our sins, and to cleanse us from all unrighteousness"
(1 John 1:7-9).

"Have mercy upon me, O God, according to thy lovingkindness: according unto the multitude of thy tender mercies blot out my transgressions. Wash me throughly from mine iniquity, and cleanse me from my sin. For I acknowledge my transgressions: and my sin is ever before me. Against thee, thee only, have I sinned, and done this evil in thy sight" (Psalm 51:1-4).

"We do not present our supplications before thee for our righteousnesses, but for thy great mercies. O Lord, hear; O Lord, forgive...And whiles I was speaking, and praying, and confessing my sin" (Daniel 9:18-20).

"And forgive us our debts, as we forgive our debtors... For if ye forgive men their trespasses, your heavenly Father

will also forgive you: But if ye forgive not men their trespasses, neither will your Father forgive your trespasses" (Matthew 6:12, 14-15).

b. We also need to ask God to help us to forgive others:

"And be ye kind one to another, tenderhearted, forgiving one another, even as God for Christ's sake hath forgiven you" (Ephesians 4:32).

"Forbearing one another, and forgiving one another, if any man have a quarrel against any: even as Christ forgave you, so also do ye" (Colossians 3:13).

When we have been hurt, disappointed, or mistreated by someone, we need God's help to genuinely forgive them. Just like God has been merciful to us and forgiven us of our sins, God expects us to also be merciful toward others and forgive them (Matthew 6:14-15; 18:21-35; Mark 11:25-26; Luke 6:37). It is very unhealthy for us to harbor unforgiveness toward others. Surely God, who does not want us to have anything in our heart against anyone else, will also give us the grace (ability, power) to forgive others from our heart.

3. Have godly sorrow for our sins (2 Corinthians 7:9-11).

We need to not just be sorry that we got caught or sorry for the consequences of some sin, but we need to be genuinely sorry that we sinned against God. Godly sorrow is something deep:

"I will declare mine iniquity; I will be sorry for my sin" (Psalm 38:18).

"Therefore also now, saith the LORD, turn ye even to me with all your heart, and with fasting, and with weeping, and with mourning: And rend your heart, and not your garments, and turn unto the LORD your God: for he is gracious and merciful, slow to anger, and of great kindness" (Joel 2:12-13).

A good example of godly sorrow is when Peter denied that he knew Jesus three times, Jesus turned and looked upon Peter, and Peter went out and wept bitterly (Luke 22:60-62). Peter was unquestionably *deeply sorry* that he had been such a disappointment to his loving Savior Jesus. It should really bother us that we have grieved or disappointed the loving God that we serve.

King David was a man after God's own heart (1 Samuel 13:14; Acts 13:22), but "displeased the LORD" (2 Sam. 11:27) when he committed adultery with Bathsheba and then had her husband Uriah killed (2 Samuel 11:1-27). Although David had to be confronted by the prophet Nathan before he repented (2 Samuel 12:1-15), David was genuinely sorry for what he had done (Psalm 51:1-17). Like King David, we should be deeply disturbed and our heart should be "broken" (Psalm 51:17) when we sin against such a wonderful, awesome, and loving God.

4. Confess our sins to others and make restitution.

a. If we have sinned against others, we need to confess our sins to them and sincerely apologize to anyone that we have hurt or mistreated. This confession should also include telling the truth if we have told lies or been dishonest in any way. Any public confession should *only be* to those that we have sinned against:

> *"And they sent a messenger unto Joseph, saying, Thy father did command before he died, saying, So shall ye say unto Joseph, Forgive, I pray thee now, the trespass of thy brethren, and their sin; for they did unto thee evil: and now, we pray thee, forgive the trespass of the servants of the God of thy father. And Joseph wept when they spake unto him. And his brethren also went and fell down before his face; and they said, Behold, we be thy servants"* *(Genesis 50:16-18).*

> *"I pray thee, forgive the trespass of thine handmaid"* *(1 Samuel 25:28).*

> *"Therefore if thou bring thy gift to the altar, and there rememberest that thy brother hath ought against thee; Leave there thy gift before the altar, and go thy way; first be reconciled to thy brother, and then come and offer thy gift."* *(Matthew 5:23-24).*

"Take heed to yourselves: If thy brother trespass against thee, rebuke him; and if he repent, forgive him. And if he trespass against thee seven times in a day, and seven times in a day turn again to thee, saying, I repent; thou shalt forgive him" (Luke 17:3-4).

"Confess your faults one to another, and pray one for another, that ye may be healed. The effectual fervent prayer of a righteous man availeth much" (James 5:16).

The word "faults" (James 5:16, KJV) is translated as "sins" (NIV).

b. Whenever possible, we need to make restitution to those affected by our sins. For example, we need to return anything that we have stolen or pay for any property damage:

"If a soul sin, and commit a trespass against the LORD, and lie unto his neighbour in that which was delivered him to keep, or in fellowship, or in a thing taken away by violence, or hath deceived his neighbour; Or have found that which was lost, and lieth concerning it, and sweareth falsely; in any of all these that a man doeth, sinning therein: Then it shall be, because he hath sinned, and is guilty, that he shall restore that which he took violently away, or the thing which he hath deceitfully gotten, or that which was delivered him to keep, or the lost thing which he found, Or all that about which he hath sworn falsely; he shall even restore it in the principal, and shall add the fifth part more thereto, and give it unto him to whom it appertaineth, in the day of his trespass offering" (Leviticus 6:2-5).

"And Zacchaeus stood, and said unto the Lord; Behold, Lord, the half of my goods I give to the poor; and if I have taken any thing from any man by false accusation, I restore him fourfold" (Luke 19:8).

5. Stop any sinful behavior and strive to please God.

It is not just a sincere decision to stop any sinful behavior in our life, but it includes doing our best to do God's will for our life. This includes both turning away from our transgressions *and* doing what is right in God's eyes (Ezekiel 18:27-30).

> *"He that covereth his sins shall not prosper: but whoso confesseth and forsaketh them shall have mercy" (Proverbs 28:13).*

> Under the subject "forsake," W.E. Vine states that in Proverbs 28:13, the words "forsaketh them" means "gives them up."[17] This signifies that whoever confesses their sins and "gives up their sins" (stops any sinful behavior) shall have mercy.

> *"Let the wicked forsake his way, and the unrighteous man his thoughts: and let him return unto the LORD, and he will have mercy upon him; and to our God, for he will abundantly pardon" (Isaiah 55:7).*

We need to not just seek a place of *forgiveness*, but instead, our sinful actions need to bother us so much that we seek God for a place of *change*. We should not be joking about or proud of any sins we have committed, but instead, we should be deeply ashamed of any sinful actions (Romans 6:21). Since God hates sin, we need to ask God to help us to hate a particular sin, or see it from His perspective.

This does not mean that we will never make mistakes. However, it does mean that we have truly given our heart to God and we want to please Him above anything else. We understand that in order to maintain our relationship with God, we need to stay clean before Him.

It is *not* saying to God, "Please forgive me, even though I am probably going to keep doing this every day." Jesus did not come to save us *in our sins*, he came to save us *from our sins* (Matthew 1:21). Jesus told the man that He healed at the pool of Bethesda, *"Behold, thou art made whole: sin no more, lest a worse thing come unto thee" (John 5:14).* Jesus told the woman that was caught in the act of adultery, *"Go, and sin no*

81

more" (John 8:11). True repentance is *not* intentionally continuing to go out and do the same sinful actions. The grace of God does not allow us to "continue in sin" (Romans 6:1-2). If we do sin, we should ask God to forgive us *and* help us to not fail again in a certain sinful way.

John the Baptist said to the multitude that came forth to be baptized of him, *"O generation of vipers, who hath warned you to flee from the wrath to come? Bring forth therefore fruits worthy of repentance" (Luke 3:7-8).* As different people asked John the Baptist, what they should do (Luke 3:10, 12, 14):

- John told the people, *"He that hath two coats, let him impart to him that hath none; and he that hath meat, let him do likewise" (Luke 3:11).*
- John told the "publicans" (Luke 3:13, KJV) or "tax collectors" (NKJV), *"Exact no more than that which is appointed you" (Luke 3:13, KJV)* or *"Don't collect any more than you are required to" (Luke 3:13, NIV).*
- John told the soldiers, *"Do violence to no man, neither accuse any falsely; and be content with your wages" (Luke 3:14, KJV)* or *"Don't extort money and don't accuse people falsely — be content with your pay" (Luke 3:14, NIV).*

In general, John was telling these people that they needed to (a) try to help others (with food and clothing, if possible), and (b) be honest and fair in their dealings with others, including not falsely accusing anyone.

Like John the Baptist, Paul preached that true repentance included turning to God and doing works "meet for" (Acts 26:20, KJV) or "befitting" (NKJV) repentance. Paul said:

"But shewed first unto them of Damascus, and at Jerusalem, and throughout all the coasts of Judaea, and then to the Gentiles, that they should repent and turn to God, and do works meet for repentance" (Acts 26:20).

"I preached that they should repent and turn to God and prove their repentance by their deeds" (Acts 26:20, NIV).

6. **Experience joy.**

Jesus does not want us to stay or remain in a sinful condition, but instead, He wants to deliver us from the bondages of sin. When we repent and our fellowship with God is restored, it should produce a feeling of joy in us. Jesus said, *"If the Son therefore shall make you free, ye shall be free indeed" (John 8:36).* There should be no more chains or guilt or condemnation to cause us to be continually depressed, but instead, there should be a joy in our soul.

After the Law of Moses was read to some Israelites from early in the morning until noon, they were convicted of their sins and they were weeping (Nehemiah 8:1-3, 9). Because it was a holy day (the Feast of Trumpets; Leviticus 23:24), Nehemiah told them to stop mourning and weeping (Nehemiah 8:9), *"For the joy of the LORD is your strength" (Nehemiah 8:10).* We need to thoroughly repent and stop any sinful behavior. But then, once we feel like we have done everything that God wants us to do to be right with Him and others, we need to put our sins behind us, go forward, and experience joy!

Paul said: *"Forgetting those things which are behind, and reaching forth unto those things which are before, I press toward the mark for the prize of the high calling of God in Christ Jesus" (Philippians 3:13-14),* and *"Rejoice in the Lord alway: and again I say, Rejoice" (Philippians 4:4).* Instead of staying focused on any sins that we have committed, our focus should be on striving to please God and doing His will.

While David was thoroughly repenting before the God that he so greatly adored, he prayed:

> *"Make me to hear joy and gladness; that the bones which thou hast broken may rejoice…Restore unto me the joy of thy salvation; and uphold me with thy free spirit" (Psalm 51:8, 12).*

Luke Chapter 15

The entire chapter of Luke 15 proclaims the joy and rejoicing that happens both on earth and in heaven (in the presence of the angels of God and our heavenly Father), when one "lost" individual is found or one sinner repents (Luke 15:6-7; 9-10). In

Luke 15:11-32, the younger son is a good example of someone that genuinely repented after living a very sinful life. This younger son took his inheritance, journeyed to a far country, spent everything that he had with riotous living, and began to be in need. While feeding pigs for a local farmer, this younger son "came to himself" (Luke 15:17):

"(17) And when he came to himself, he said, How many hired servants of my father's have bread enough and to spare, and I perish with hunger! (18) I will arise and go to my father, and will say unto him, Father, I have sinned against heaven, and before thee, (19) And am no more worthy to be called thy son: make me as one of thy hired servants. (20) And he arose, and came to his father. But when he was yet a great way off, his father saw him, and had compassion, and ran, and fell on his neck, and kissed him. (21) And the son said unto him, Father, I have sinned against heaven, and in thy sight, and am no more worthy to be called thy son. (22) But the father said to his servants, Bring forth the best robe, and put it on him; and put a ring on his hand, and shoes on his feet: (23) And bring hither the fatted calf, and kill it; and let us eat, and be merry: (24) For this my son was dead, and is alive again; he was lost, and is found. And they began to be merry. (25) Now his elder son was in the field: and as he came and drew nigh to the house, he heard musick and dancing" (Luke 15:17-25).

Not only did this younger son, have a change of mind and heart, but he also had a complete change of direction. Instead of continuing to live a sinful life, he decided to return to his loving father and confess all of his sins (Luke 15:17-20). His loving father saw his "lost" son when he was still a long way from home, ran to him, embraced him, fell on his neck, gave him a kiss, restored him as a son, and celebrated his return (Luke 15:20-25).

The actions of this loving father can be likened to the actions of our loving heavenly Father, when one of His wayward children decide to return to Him. A celebration occurs when someone "dead in their trespasses and sins" (Ephesians 2:1) is restored to life and fellowship with God (Luke 15:22-25, 32).

9 - <u>Water Baptism</u>

<u>Water Baptism Is Necessary for Our Salvation</u>

Water baptism is a scriptural command and is necessary for our salvation. Jesus said to His apostles:

> *"He that believeth and is baptized shall be saved; but he that believeth not shall be damned" (Mark 16:16).*

Water baptism is not a human work, but rather, it is part of God's New Testament plan of salvation. A person shows their faith in God to save them, when they obey the command of Jesus to be baptized. An individual believes that when they go down into the water in the name of Jesus and come up out of it, their past record of sins has been washed away by the blood of Jesus.

Jesus said:

> *"Verily, verily, I say unto thee, Except a man be born of water and of the Spirit, he cannot enter into the kingdom of God" (John 3:5).*

We must be "born of water," which refers to "being baptized in water" to become a member of the New Testament "kingdom of God" (or New Testament Church).

Peter wrote:

> *"Which sometime were disobedient, when once the longsuffering of God waited in the days of Noah, while the ark was a preparing, wherein few, that is, eight souls were saved by water. The like figure whereunto even baptism doth also now save us (not the putting away of the filth of the flesh, but the answer of a good conscience toward God,) by the resurrection of Jesus Christ" (1 Peter 3:20-21).*

When we are baptized in Jesus' name, the blood of Jesus is applied to our life and our sins are forgiven by God. This should give us a "good" (1 Peter 3:21) or a cleansed conscience: *"How much more shall the blood of Christ, who through the eternal Spirit offered himself without spot to God, purge your conscience from dead works to serve the living God?" (Hebrews 9:14).* The word "purge" (Hebrews 9:14, KJV) is translated as "cleanse" (NKJV).

People Baptized in the Book of Acts

Nine Examples of People Being Baptized in Water in the Book of Acts:	
Account	**Scriptures**
Peter and the eleven apostles to Jews	*"Then Peter said unto them, Repent, and be baptized every one of you in the name of Jesus Christ for the remission of sins"* (Acts 2:38). *"Then they that gladly received his word were baptized: and the same day there were added unto them about three thousand souls"* *(Acts 2:41).*
Philip to Samaritans	Men and women of Samaria that believed Philip's preaching *"were baptized in the name of the Lord Jesus"* *(Acts 8:16).*
Philip to the Ethiopian eunuch	The Ethiopian eunuch (a) believed Philip's preaching about Jesus (Acts 8:30-35), (b) requested to be baptized as they came to some water (Acts 8:36), (c) was told by Philip that he could be baptized if he believed with all of his heart (Acts 8:37), (d) told Philip *"I believe that Jesus Christ is the Son of God"* *(Acts 8:37),* and (e) was baptized by full immersion in water (Acts 8:38-39).
Ananias to Paul	Ananias told Paul *"And now why tarriest thou? Arise, and be baptized, and wash away thy sins, calling on the name of the Lord"* (Acts 22:16). Paul *"was baptized"* (Acts 9:18).
Peter to Cornelius & other Gentiles	Peter said: *"Can any man forbid water, that these should not be baptized, which have received the Holy Ghost as well as we? And he commanded them to be baptized in the name of the Lord"* (Acts 10:47-48).

Nine Examples of People Being Baptized in Water in the Book of Acts (continued):	
Account	**Scriptures**
Paul & Silas to Lydia and the jailer in Philippi	Paul & Silas preached the gospel (Acts 16:10) in Philippi. After believing their preaching: (a) Lydia and her household were baptized (Acts 16:14-15), and (b) The jailer and his household were immediately baptized (Acts 16:30-34).
Paul to the Corinthians	*"And Crispus, the chief ruler of the synagogue, believed on the Lord with all his house; and many of the Corinthians hearing believed, and were baptized" (Acts 18:8).*
Paul to twelve disciples of John the Baptist at Ephesus	John the Baptist preached that people should repent and confess their sins before he baptized them by full immersion in water (Mark 1:4-5). John the Baptist was beheaded (Matthew 14:1-12) *before* Jesus died for the sins of the world. John the Baptist did not baptize people in the name of Jesus for the remission of their sins, because this New Testament plan of salvation did not go into effect until *after* Jesus died for our sins (Hebrews 9:16-17). Perhaps you would think that Paul could just pray for these repented disciples that had been baptized by John the Baptist, but that is not what Paul did (Acts 19:1-7). Paul understood the importance of the name of Jesus (Colossians 3:17; Acts 4:12). Paul rebaptized these disciples *"in the name of the Lord Jesus" (Acts 19:5).*

Here are some conclusions that we can see from these examples in the book of Acts:

1. **We must repent *before* we are baptized for the remission (forgiveness) of our sins (Acts 2:38).** Our sins are still with us until we are baptized in Jesus' name and wash away our sins (Acts 22:16).

As the song "Nothing But the Blood" by Robert Lowry states: "What can wash away my sin? Nothing but the blood of Jesus. What can make me whole again? Nothing but the blood of Jesus." The blood of Jesus (a) cleanses us when repent and confess our sins (1 John 1:7-9), and (b) remits (forgives) our sins when we repent and are baptized in water in the name of Jesus (Acts 2:38). The *only* reason that we can have our sins remitted (forgiven) is because Jesus Christ "died for our sins" (1 Corinthians 15:3):

> Jesus said, *"For this is my blood of the new testament, which is shed for many for the remission of sins" (Matthew 26:28).*

> Paul wrote, *"And almost all things are by the law purged with blood; and without shedding of blood is no remission" (Hebrews 9:22).*

2. **In all nine examples, individuals "heard" and "believed" the Acts 2:38 message of salvation *before* they were baptized.** This is why infant baptism is not scriptural. An infant cannot repent or believe.

Philip preached unto those in Samaria: (a) "Christ" (Acts 8:5), and (b) *"The things concerning the kingdom of God, and the name of Jesus Christ" (Acts 8:12)*. Since the Samaritans and Simon the sorcerer "believed" (Acts 8:12, 13) and were *"baptized in the name of the Lord Jesus" (Acts 8:16)*, Philip must have said something to them about their need to be baptized in the name of Jesus to have the blood of Jesus wash away (or remit, forgive) their sins.

Philip preached unto the Ethiopian eunuch that the slain lamb in Isaiah 53:7-8 was a man called Jesus (Acts 8:30-35). Since the eunuch said *"See, here is water; what doth hinder me to be baptized?" (Acts 8:36)*, Philip must have said something to the eunuch about his need to be baptized in water to have his sins washed away. Then Philip said, *"If thou believest with all thine heart, thou mayest" (Acts 8:37)*. The eunuch answered Philip *"I believe that Jesus Christ is the Son of God" (Acts 8:37)*. The eunuch commanded the chariot to stand still and Philip baptized the eunuch (Acts 8:38-39).

3. **After the birth of the New Testament Church in Acts chapter 2, they were baptized as soon as they understood this scriptural command (John 3:5; Mark 16:16; 1 Peter 3:20-21).**

In Acts 2:41, three thousand people, which gladly received what Peter preached, were baptized "the same day."

In Acts 8:35-39, the Ethiopian eunuch was baptized as soon as he understood the New Testament plan of salvation shown to him by Philip.

In Acts 9:17-18, after Ananias prayed for Paul, he received his sight, and "arose, and was baptized." Ananias had told Paul *"And now why tarriest thou? Arise, and be baptized, and wash away thy sins, calling on the name of the Lord." (Acts 22:16).* The words "why tarriest thou?" (Acts 22:16, KJV) are translated as "why are you waiting?" (NKJV). It appears that Paul was baptized in water as soon as he understood the New Testament plan of salvation explained to him by Ananias.

In Acts 10, after Cornelius and other Gentiles were filled with the Holy Ghost, what happened? Peter commanded them to be baptized in water in the name of the Lord (Acts 10:47-48).

In Acts 16:27-34, Paul and Silas preached the New Testament plan of salvation to the Philippian jailer and his household sometime after midnight. The Philippian jailer and his household were "immediately" baptized (Acts 16:33, NKJV).

4. **The proper mode for water baptism is by full immersion in water.**

"And he commanded the chariot to stand still: and they went down both into the water, both Philip and the eunuch; and he baptized him. And when they were come up out of the water, the Spirit of the Lord caught away Philip, that the eunuch saw him no more: and he went on his way rejoicing" (Acts 8:38-39).

In the Gospels (Matthew, Mark, Luke, and John), book of Acts, and all New Testament Epistles (a) the word "baptize" (and "baptized" or "baptizing") is translated from the Greek word *baptizo*, which means "to immerse, submerge; to make overwhelmed (i.e. fully wet)," and (b) the word "baptism" is translated from the Greek word *baptisma*, which means "immersion." When Acts 8:38 states "he baptized him," this means that Phillip completely immersed the body of the Ethiopian eunuch in water.

The Greek word *rhantizo*, which means "to sprinkle," is *never* translated as baptism, baptized, baptize, or baptizing in the Bible. The Greek word *rhantizo* only appears four times in the Bible and is translated as "sprinkling" in Hebrews 9:13, and as "sprinkled" in Hebrews 9:19, 9:21, 10:22. If God meant for Christian water baptism to be done by having water *sprinkled* on us, then the Greek word *rhantizo* should have been used when people were baptized, instead of the Greek words *baptizo* or *baptisma*.

Every time that John the Baptist or the early church baptized someone, it was by immersion (fully submerging their entire body in water). They needed "much water" (John 3:23) to baptize people by immersion:

> *"And John also was baptizing in Aenon near to Salim, because there was much water there: and they came, and were baptized" (John 3:23).*

Although Jesus was "without sin" (Hebrews 4:15), Jesus wanted everyone to know that He endorsed John the Baptist's ministry. Jesus, our example in all things, was baptized by having his entire body completely immersed in water:

> *"And Jesus, when he was baptized, went up straightway out of the water: and, lo, the heavens were opened unto him, and he saw the Spirit of God descending like a dove, and lighting upon him" (Matthew 3:16).*

The word "straightway" (Matthew 3:16, KJV) is translated as "immediately" (NKJV).

Similar to Jesus' death and burial, we have to have our own death (repentance) and burial (water baptism). Water baptism is our "burial" with Jesus Christ. When we are baptized (immersed) in water in the name of Jesus, we are "buried with him" (Romans 6:4; Colossians 2:12):

"(3) Know ye not, that so many of us as were baptized into Jesus Christ were baptized into his death? (4) Therefore we are buried with him by baptism into death: that like as Christ was raised up from the dead by the glory of the Father, even so we also should walk in newness of life. (5) For if we have been planted together in the likeness of his death, we shall be also in the likeness of his resurrection" (Romans 6:3-5).

"(11) In whom also ye are circumcised with the circumcision made without hands, in putting off the body of the sins of the flesh by the circumcision of Christ: (12) Buried with him in baptism, wherein also ye are risen with him through the faith of the operation of God, who hath raised him from the dead. (13) And you, being dead in your sins and the uncircumcision of your flesh, hath he quickened together with him, having forgiven you all trespasses" *(Colossians 2:11-13).*

5. **The proper formula for water baptism is "in the name of Jesus" (Acts 2:38; 8:16; 10:48; 19:5; 22:16; see also Acts 4:10-12; Colossians 3:17).** Lord and Christ are titles for Jesus and can also be spoken (with the name Jesus) when baptizing someone.

Peter to the Jews in Jerusalem: *"Repent, and be baptized every one of you in the name of Jesus Christ for the remission of sins" (Acts 2:38).*

Phillip to the Samaritans: *"(For as yet he was fallen upon none of them: only they were baptized in the name of the Lord Jesus)" (Acts 8:16).*

Peter to the Gentiles: *"And he commanded them to be baptized in the name of the Lord" (Acts 10:48).* The words "baptized in the name of the Lord" (Acts 10:48, KJV) are translated as "baptized in the name of Jesus Christ" (NIV).

Paul to the Ephesians: *"When they heard this, they were baptized in the name of the Lord Jesus" (Acts 19:5).*

Ananias to Paul: *"And now why tarriest thou? Arise, and be baptized, and wash away thy sins, calling on the name of the Lord" (Acts 22:16).* The words "and wash away thy sins, calling on the name of the Lord" (Acts 22:16, KJV) are translated as "and by calling upon His name, wash away your sins" (AMPCE).

Peter said, *"Be it known unto you all, and to all the people of Israel, that by the name of Jesus Christ of Nazareth, whom ye crucified, whom God raised from the dead, even by him doth this man stand here before you whole. This is the stone which was set at nought of you builders, which is become the head of the corner. Neither is there salvation in any other: for there is none other name under heaven given among men, whereby we must be saved" (Acts 4:10-12).* Why did the apostles baptize in the name of Jesus? Because it is the only name under heaven given among men, whereby we must be saved.

Paul wrote, *"And whatsoever ye do in word or deed, do all in the name of the Lord Jesus, giving thanks to God and the Father by him" (Colossians 3:17).* We should do all of the following in the name of Jesus: gather together (Matthew 18:20), make prayer requests (John 14:14; 15:16; 16:23), pray for healing (Mark 16:17-18; James 5:14-15), cast out demons (Mark 16:17; Acts 16:18), and baptize people in water (Acts 2:38; 8:16; 10:48; 19:5; 22:16).

Paul was a Jew (Acts 22:3) that believed in one God whose name is Jehovah (Deuteronomy 6:4). Paul was blinded by a light from heaven on the road to Damascus and he heard a voice say to him *"Saul, Saul, why persecutest thou me?" (Acts 9:4).* Paul asked the question *"Who art thou, Lord?" (Acts 9:5)* or "Who are you Jehovah (one God of Israel)?" In this encounter with God, Paul saw a vision of the resurrected Christ (Acts 22:14; 1 Corinthians 15:8) and the Lord answered Paul *"I am Jesus" (Acts 9:5).* God revealed Himself to Paul as Jesus Christ, his Saviour (Titus 1:3-4; 2:10, 13; 3:4, 6). Paul later wrote that Jesus Christ is the image of the invisible God (Colossians 1:15; 2 Corinthians 4:4). Paul understood that Jesus is a name, which is above every name (Philippians 2:9-11; Ephesians 1:21).

<u>Matthew 28:19</u>

"Go ye therefore, and teach all nations, baptizing them in the name of the Father, and of the Son, and of the Holy Ghost" (Matthew 28:19).

Father, Son, and Holy Ghost are titles. There is no power in titles. This verse does not say names (plural), but rather it says name (singular). How did the apostles baptize? In the name of Jesus (Acts 2:38; 8:16; 10:48; 19:5; 22:16).

Jesus is the name of the Son. *"And she shall bring forth a son, and **thou shalt call his name JESUS**: for he shall save his people from their sins. Now all this was done, that it might be fulfilled which was spoken of the Lord by the prophet, saying, Behold, a virgin shall be with child, and shall bring forth a son, and they shall call his name Emmanuel, which being interpreted is, God with us" (Matthew 1:21-23).*

Jesus is the name of the Father. *"For unto us a child is born, unto us a son is given: and the government shall be upon his shoulder: and **his name shall be called** Wonderful, Counsellor, The mighty God, **The everlasting Father**, The Prince of Peace" (Isaiah 9:6).* In Isaiah 9:6: (a) "child" and "son" refer to the humanity of Jesus Christ, (b) "mighty God" and "everlasting Father" refer to His deity. Jesus was the one God of the Old Testament (or Father, Spirit of God) robed in the body of Jesus Christ.

The book of Psalms states that the Messiah (or Christ) would declare God's name: *"(19) O LORD... (22) I will declare **thy name** unto my brethren" (Psalms 22:19, 22).* The New Testament states: *"(9) But we see Jesus... (12) Saying, I will declare **thy name** unto my brethren." (Hebrews 2:9, 12).* The words *"thy name" (Hebrews 2:12, KJV)* is also translated as *"**Your [the Father's] name**" (Hebrew 2:12, AMPCE).*

Jesus said: *"I am come **in my Father's name**" (John 5:43), "(5) O Father... (6) I have manifested **thy name**... (26) And I have declared unto them **thy name**" (John 17:5, 6, 26).* Where did Jesus get his name? From his Father. Jesus is described as: *"Being made so much better than the angels, as he hath **by inheritance obtained a more excellent name than they**" (Hebrews 1:4).*

Jesus is the name of the Holy Ghost. Jesus said: *"And I will pray the Father, and he shall give you another Comforter, that he may abide with you for ever; Even the Spirit of truth; whom the world cannot receive, because it seeth him not, neither knoweth him: but ye know him; for he dwelleth with you, and shall be in you.* **I will not leave you comfortless: I will come to you**" *(John 14:16-18)*, and *"But the Comforter, which is the Holy Ghost, whom the Father will send* **in my name**" *(John 14:26).*

The Holy Spirit is referred to as *"**the Spirit of God**" (Gen. 1:2; Job 33:4; Romans 8:9)*, *"**My Spirit**" (Gen. 6:3; Joel 2:28; NKJV)*, *"**the Spirit of the LORD**" (Isaiah 59:19; Ezek. 11:5)*, *"**the Spirit of the Lord**" (Luke 4:18; 2 Cor. 3:17, 18)*, *"**the Spirit of your Father**" (Matt 10:20)*, *"**the Spirit of Jesus**" (Acts 16:7; NIV)*, *"**the Spirit of his Son**" (Gal. 4:6)*, *"**the Spirit of Jesus Christ**" (Phil. 1:19)*, and *"**the Spirit of Christ**" (Rom. 8:9; 1 Peter 1:11).*

The Bible is very clear that the "Holy Ghost" (Matthew 1:18, Luke 1:35, KJV) or "Holy Spirit" (NKJV) was the Father of Jesus: *"Now the birth of Jesus Christ was on this wise: When as his mother Mary was espoused to Joseph, before they came together, she was found with* **child of the Holy Ghost**" *(Matthew 1:18).* *"And the angel answered and said unto her,* **The Holy Ghost shall come upon thee**, *and the power of the Highest shall overshadow thee: therefore also that holy thing which shall be born of thee shall be called the Son of God" (Luke 1:35).*

Did Jesus have two fathers? The Father and the Holy Spirit? No. The Bible is clear that there is only one God (Deuteronomy 6:4; Galatians 3:20; James 2:19), who is holy (Leviticus 19:2) and a Spirit (John 4:24). God is a Holy Spirit. "Holy Spirit" and "Holy Ghost" are synonymous terms. The Holy Ghost is *God in action* or *God as He works among mankind.*

Simply stated, the one Spirit of God has three offices: the Father in creation, the Son in redemption, and the Holy Ghost in regeneration or as He works among mankind.

Jesus is the New Testament revealed name of God. All miracles, signs, wonders, and healings are done by the name of Jesus (Acts 3:6, 16; 4:10, 30; 9:34). Jesus is the only name under heaven given among men by which we can be saved (Acts 4:12).

Jesus is the Name "of the Son" and "of the Father" and "of the Holy Ghost"	
Question	**Answer**
Who did John the Baptist prepare the way for?	**Jehovah** (Isaiah 40:3-5; Malachi 3:1); **Jesus** (Matthew 3:1-3; Mark 1:2-3; Luke 3:2-6; John 1:19, 23).
Who is our loving Shepherd?	**Jehovah** (Psalm 23:1; 80:1; 100:3); **Jesus** (John 10:11, 14-16; Hebrews 13:20; 1 Peter 5:4).
Whose hands, feet, and side were pierced?	**Jehovah** (Zechariah 12:10); **Jesus** (Psalm 22:16; Luke 24:40; John 19:33-37; 20:19-20, 24-28; Rev. 1:7).
Who raised the man Jesus Christ from the dead?	**God** (Acts 2:24, 32; 10:39-40; 13:30; 1 Cor. 15:15; Col. 2:12; 1 Pet. 1:21); **The Father** (Romans 6:4; Galatians 1:1); **Jesus** (John 2:19-21); **The Spirit of God** (Romans 8:9-11; 1 Peter 3:18).
Who gives people the gift of the Holy Ghost?	**Jehovah** (Joel 2:27-29); **God** (Acts 2:17-18; 5:32; 11:16-17; 15:8; 2 Corinthians 5:5; Galatians 4:6; 1 Thes. 4:8; 1 John 3:24; 4:12-13); **The Father** (Luke 11:13; John 14:16, 26); **Jesus** (Matt. 3:11; Mark 1:8; Luke 3:16; 24:49; John 1:33; 7:37-39; 15:26; 16:7); **The Spirit** (1 Corinthians 12:13).
When you receive the Holy Ghost, you are the temple of Whom?	**God** (1 Corinthians 3:16-17; 2 Corinthians 6:16); **The Holy Ghost** (1 Corinthians 6:19).
When you receive the Holy Ghost, Who dwells in you?	**The Spirit of God** (1 Corinthians 3:16; Romans 8:9, 11); **The Spirit of your Father** (Matthew 10:20; Ephesians 3:14-16; 4:6); **The Spirit of Christ** (Rom. 8:9-10; 2 Cor. 13:5; Gal. 2:20; Eph. 3:17; Col. 1:27); **The Holy Ghost** (1 Cor 6:19; 2 Tim. 1:14).

95

Jesus is the Name "of the Son" and "of the Father" and "of the Holy Ghost" (continued)	
Question	**Answer**
Who gives you the words to speak when you are brought before rulers and kings for Jesus' sake?	**The Spirit of your Father** (Matthew 10:18-20); **Jesus** (Luke 21:12-15); **The Holy Ghost** (Mark 13:9, 11).
Who is coming back to the Mount of Olives with all His saints?	**Jehovah** (Zechariah 14:3-5, 9)**;** **Jesus** (Acts 1:9-12; 1 Thessalonians 3:13; Revelation 19:11-21).
Who answers prayer?	**Jehovah** (Psalm 34:15, 17; 2 Chronicles 7:12-14); **God** (Psalm 65:2); **The Father** (Matthew 6:6; 18:19; John 15:16; 16:23); **Jesus** (John 14:13-14; Acts 7:59-60).
Who is the Almighty God or God Almighty?	**Jehovah** (Gen. 17:1; Exodus 6:3); **God** (Gen. 35:11; Job 5:17); **The Father** (2 Cor. 6:17-18); **Jesus** (Revelation 1:8; 4:8); **The Spirit of God** (Job 33:4).
Who is the First and the Last?	**Jehovah** (Isaiah 44:6; 48:12); **Jesus** (Revelation 1:11, 17; 2:8; 22:13).
Who sent His angel to show John the book of Revelation	**God** (Revelation 1:1); **The Lord God of the holy prophets** (Revelation 22:6); **Jesus** (Revelation 22:16).
Who is our Judge?	**Jehovah** (Isaiah 33:22); **God** (Psalm 50:6; Hebrews 12:23; Revelation 20:11-12); **Jesus** (Romans 2:16; 14:10-12; Acts 10:42; 17:31; 2 Timothy 4:1).
Every knee shall bow and every tongue shall confess to Whom?	**Jehovah** (Isaiah 45:21-23); **Jesus** (Philippians 2:9-11; Romans 14:11).

The Right Hand of God

The New Testament mentions Jesus sitting (Mark 16:19; Colossians 3:1; Hebrews 10:12) or standing (Acts 7:55-56) on "the right hand of God." It also mentions Jesus being at (Romans 8:34) or on (1 Peter 3:22) "the right hand of God." What does the phrase "right hand of God" mean? Since God is an omnipresent invisible Spirit (Jeremiah 23:24; 1 Timothy 1:17), how do you get on His right hand? Some of God's actions use symbolic language:

> *"And with the blast of thy nostrils the waters were gathered together, the floods stood upright as an heap, and the depths were congealed in the heart of the sea" (Exodus 15:8).* They did not see a huge nose in the sky, but instead, they saw God part the waters of the Red Sea by a strong wind (Exodus 14:21).

> *"The eyes of the LORD are in every place, beholding the evil and the good" (Proverbs 15:3).* There are not literal eyes everywhere, but instead, God is omnipresent. God sees and knows everything going on in the world.

In the Bible, "the right hand of God" does not refer to a physical body part or geographical position, but instead, it can be figurative language referring to God's power or strength:

> *"Thy right hand, O LORD, is become glorious in power: thy right hand, O LORD, hath dashed in pieces the enemy" (Exodus 15:6).*

> *"Thy right hand hath holden me up" (Psalm 18:35).*

> *"Now know I that the LORD saveth his anointed; he will hear him from his holy heaven with the saving strength of his right hand" (Psalm 20:6).*

> *"(32) This Jesus hath God raised up, whereof we all are witnesses. (33) Therefore being by the right hand of God exalted" (Acts 2:32-33).*

According to W.E. Vine, the words "right hand" (Greek: *dexios*) in Acts 2:33 is:

> An adjective, used...metaphorically of "power" or "authority"[18]

Jesus Christ told the Jewish religious leaders:

> *"Hereafter shall the Son of man sit on the right hand of the power of God" (Luke 22:69)*, and *"Hereafter shall ye see the Son of man sitting on the right hand of power, and coming in the clouds of heaven" (Matthew 26:64)*.

After Jesus Christ rose from the dead, He showed Himself to His disciples in his glorified immortal body (1 Corinthians 15:5-7, 52; John 20:19-29; 21:4-22). During this time, Jesus said to His disciples: *"All power is given unto me in heaven and in earth" (Matthew 28:18)*. Jesus Christ ascended up to heaven in His glorified human body (Acts 1:9-11). Jesus Christ has now been "exalted" (Philippians 2:9) to be at "the right hand of God," which is figurative language signifying that Jesus Christ has all of the power and authority of God:

> Peter wrote, *"Who is gone into heaven, and is on the right hand of God; angels and authorities and powers being made subject unto him" (1 Peter 3:22)*.

> Paul wrote that God raised Christ *"from the dead, and set him at his own right hand in the heavenly places, Far above all principality, and power, and might, and dominion, and every name that is named, not only in this world, but also in that which is to come" (Ephesians 1:20-21)*.

As Stephen was being stoned to death, he was *"calling upon God, and saying, Lord Jesus, receive my spirit" (Acts 7:59)*. What did Stephen see? The Bible says that he *"saw the glory of God and Jesus standing on the right hand of God" (Acts 7:55)*. Stephen said: *"Behold, I see the heavens opened, and the Son of man standing on the right hand of God" (Acts 7:56)*. Stephen saw *"the glory of God in the face of Jesus Christ" (2 Corinthians 4:6)*. He only saw Jesus Christ, *"Who is the image of the invisible God" (Colossians 1:15)*. He only saw Jesus Christ in His glorified human body with all of the power and authority of God. This is why he called upon God saying, "Lord Jesus" (Acts 7:59).

When we get to heaven and stand before God, Who will we see? We will see Jesus Christ in his glorified human body (Revelation 22:4), who is the "everlasting Father" (Isaiah 9:6) and "the Almighty' (Revelation 1:8).

10 - <u>The Gift of the Holy Ghost</u>

<u>Different Descriptions for Receiving the Holy Ghost</u>

The same experience of "receiving the gift of the Holy Ghost" (Acts 2:38) is described in different ways.

1. <u>Gift (Greek: **dorea**):</u>
   (a) *"Ye shall receive the **gift** of the Holy Ghost" (Acts 2:38)*,
   (b) *"The **gift** of God" (Acts 8:20)*, (c) *"Was poured out the **gift** of the Holy Ghost. For they heard them speak in tongues, and magnify God" (Acts 10:45-46)*, and (d) *"God gave them the like **gift** as he did unto us, who believed on the Lord Jesus Christ" (Acts 11:17)*.

2. <u>**Promise:**</u>
   (a*) "I send the **promise** of my Father upon you...endued with power from on high" (Luke 24:49)*, (b) *"The **promise** of the Father" (Acts 1:4)*, (c) *"Having received of the Father the **promise** of the Holy Ghost...which ye now see and hear" (Acts 2:33)*, (d) *"The **promise**" (Acts 2:39)*, (e) *"That we might receive the **promise** of the Spirit through faith" (Galatians 3:14)*, and (f) *"Sealed with that holy Spirit of **promise**" (Ephesians 1:13)*.

3. <u>**Baptize (or baptized, baptizeth):**</u>
   (a) *"He shall **baptize** you with the Holy Ghost and with fire" (Matthew 3:11; Luke 3:16)*, (b) *"He shall **baptize** you with the Holy Ghost" (Mark 1:8)*, (c) *"He which **baptizeth** with the Holy Ghost" (John 1:33)*, and (d) *"**Baptized** with the Holy Ghost" (Acts 1:5; 11:16)*.

4. <u>**Come (or come upon, came on):**</u>
   (a) *"I will not leave you comfortless: I will **come** to you" (John 14:18)*, (b) *"But when the Comforter is **come**, whom I will send unto you from the Father, even the Spirit of truth, which proceedeth from the Father, he shall testify of me" (John 15:26)*, (c) *"Nevertheless I tell you the truth; it is expedient for you that I go away: for if I go not away, the Comforter will not **come** unto you; but if I depart, I will send him unto you. And when he is **come**, he will reprove the world of sin, and of righteousness, and of judgment...Howbeit when he, the Spirit*

*of truth, is **come**, he will guide you into all truth: for he shall not speak of himself; but whatsoever he shall hear, that shall he speak: and he will shew you things to come. He shall glorify me" (John 16:7-8, 13-14),* (d) *"But ye shall receive power after that the Holy Ghost is **come upon** you" (Acts 1:8),* and (e) *"The Holy Ghost **came on** them; and they spake with tongues, and prophesied" (Acts 19:6).*

5. **Fell on:**
   (a) *"The Holy Ghost **fell on** all them which heard the word" (Acts 10:44),* and (b) *"As I began to speak, the Holy Ghost **fell on** them, as on us at the beginning" (Acts 11:15).*

6. **Filled with:**
   (a) *"**Filled with** the Holy Ghost, and began to speak with other tongues, as the Spirit gave them utterance" (Acts 2:4),* and (b) *"Be **filled with** the Holy Ghost" (Acts 9:17).*

7. **Give (or gave, given, giving):**
   (a) *"How much more shall your heavenly Father **give** the Holy Spirit to them that ask him?" (Luke 11:13),* (b) *"Jesus stood and cried, saying, If any man thirst, let him come unto me, and drink. He that believeth on me, as the scripture hath said, out of his belly shall flow rivers of living water. (But this spake he of the Spirit, which they that believe on him should receive: for the Holy Ghost was not yet **given**; because that Jesus was not yet glorified.)" (John 7:37-39),* (c) *"And I will pray the Father, and he shall **give** you another Comforter, that he may abide with you for ever; Even the Spirit of truth...he dwelleth with you, and shall be in you...But the Comforter, which is the Holy Ghost, whom the Father will send in my name, he shall teach you all things, and bring all things to your remembrance, whatsoever I have said unto you" (John 14:16-17, 26),* (d) *"The Holy Ghost, whom God **hath given** to them that obey him" (Acts 5:32),* (e) *"The Holy Ghost **was given**" (Acts 8:18),* (f) *"God **gave** them the like gift as he did unto us who believed on the Lord Jesus Christ" (Acts 11:17),* and (g) *"God...**giving** them the Holy Ghost, even as he did unto us" (Acts 15:8).*

8. **Pour (or poured) out:**
   (a) *God said "I will **pour out**...of my Spirit" (Acts 2:17,18),* and (b) *"Was **poured out** the gift of the Holy Ghost. For they heard them speak with tongues, and magnify God" (Acts 10:45-46).*

9. **Received (or receive):**
   (a) *"Having **received** of the Father the promise of the Holy Ghost...which ye now see and hear" (Acts 2:33),* (b) *"Ye shall **receive** the gift of the Holy Ghost" (Acts 2:38),* (c) *"They **received** the Holy Ghost" (Acts 8:17),* (d) *"**Receive** the Holy Ghost" (Acts 8:19),* and (e) *"Have ye **received** the Holy Ghost since ye believed?" (Acts 19:2).*

Purposes of the Holy Ghost

When we receive the gift of the Holy Ghost, the "Spirit of Christ" in us will help us in many ways. The Holy Ghost in us will:

1. Give us power (Luke 24:49; Acts 1:8) to be a victorious witness and overcomer in this world (Hebrews 4:15; Romans 8:1-17; 1 John 4:4; 5:4-5; Revelation 2:7, 11, 17, 26; 3:5, 12, 21; 21:7).
2. Teach us all things (John 14:26).
3. Testify of Jesus Christ (John 15:26).
4. Guide us into all truth (John 16:13).
5. Show us things to come (John 16:13).
6. Glorify Jesus Christ (John 16:14).
7. "Abide" (KJV) or "be" (NIV) with us for ever (John 14:16).

The Holy Spirit of Promise

Paul wrote, *"(13) In whom ye also trusted, after that ye heard the word of truth, the gospel of your salvation: in whom also after that ye believed, ye were sealed with that holy Spirit of promise, (14) Which is the earnest of our inheritance until the redemption of the purchased possession, unto the praise of his glory" (Ephesians 1:13-14).*

First, we hear about the gift of the Holy Spirit (or Holy Ghost). Then we understand that God greatly desires for us to have this gift. Then we seek God for this gift and are sealed with the Holy

Spirit. Notice Ephesians 1:13 says "Holy Spirit of promise." Why? Because God has promised to give the Holy Spirit to all those that will sincerely seek Him for this gift.

The Holy Spirit is a free gift, which is received by faith. It is by the grace of God (or unmerited favor of God) that we are able to receive this precious gift. It is the nature of God to pour out blessings and gifts upon us and His nature will never change (James 1:17).

The Holy Spirit is the "earnest of our inheritance" (Ephesians 1:14, KJV), which is also translated as the "guarantee of our inheritance [the firstfruits, the pledge and foretaste, the down payment on our heritage]" (AMPCE).

People received the gift of the Holy Ghost for the first time in Acts chapter 2. There are several other accounts in the book of Acts when someone was filled with the Holy Ghost. We will examine these other accounts in this chapter.

Philip to the Samaritans
(Acts 8:5-24)

Philip preached unto those in Samaria: "Christ" (Acts 8:5), and *"The things concerning the kingdom of God, and the name of Jesus Christ" (Acts 8:12)*. The following miracles and signs were heard and seen (Acts 8:6, 13): (a) *"Unclean spirits, crying with loud voice, came out of many that were possessed with them" (Acts 8:7)*, (b) Many people that were paralyzed or crippled were healed (Acts 8:7), and (c) *"There was great joy in that city" (Acts 8:8)*.

The people of Samaria believed Philip's preaching and were baptized in water in the name of the Lord Jesus, but had *not yet* received the Holy Ghost (Acts 8:12-13, 15-16). The apostles Peter and John were sent from Jerusalem to pray that these Samaritans would receive the gift of the Holy Ghost (Acts 8:14-15). When these two apostles laid their hands on these Samaritans, *they received the Holy Ghost and there was some external sign given* (Acts 8:17). Simon the sorcerer, who had believed and been baptized, wanted to buy "this power" for people to receive the Holy Ghost when he laid his hands on them (Acts 8:18-19). Peter told Simon the sorcerer that "the gift of God" (receiving the Holy Ghost) could not be purchased with money (Acts 8:20-24).

Peter to Cornelius & Other Gentiles in Caesarea (Acts 10:1-48; 11:1-18; 15:7-11)

Acts 10:1-4, 30-31: In Caesarea, there was a Roman centurion named Cornelius (Acts 10:1). He was, *"A devout man, and one that feared God with all his house, which gave much alms to the people, and prayed to God alway" (Acts 10:2).* The word "alway" (Acts 10:2; KJV) is translated as "always" (NKJV) or "regularly" (NIV). While Cornelius was praying at "about the ninth hour of the day" (3:00 PM), he saw an angel of God in a vision (Acts 10:3; 30). The angel told Cornelius *"Thy prayers and thine alms are come up for a memorial before God" (Acts 10:4).*

Acts 10:5-8, 24, 32-33; 11:11-14: Cornelius was told by the angel from God to send for Peter, *"Who shall tell thee words, whereby thou and all thy house shall be saved" (Acts 11:14).* The word "house" (Acts 11:14, KJV) is translated as "household" (NKJV). Peter came to Caesarea with six Jewish Christian brothers (Acts 11:12) and spoke to Cornelius and those Gentiles with him, including all of his "household" (Acts 11:14, NKJV), and "his relatives and close friends" (Acts 10:24, NKJV).

Acts 10:44-48, 11:15-18, and 15:7-11 use different words to describe what happened when Peter preached to Cornelius and other Gentiles:

"(44) While Peter yet spake these words, the Holy Ghost fell on all them which heard the word. (45) And they of the circumcision which believed were astonished, as many as came with Peter, because that on the Gentiles also was poured out the gift of the Holy Ghost. (46) For they heard them speak with tongues, and magnify God. Then answered Peter, (47) Can any man forbid water, that these should not be baptized, which have received the Holy Ghost as well as we? (48) And he commanded them to be baptized in the name of the Lord. Then prayed they him to tarry certain days" (Acts 10:44-48).

"(15) And as I began to speak, the Holy Ghost fell on them, as on us at the beginning. (16) Then remembered I the word of the Lord, how that he said, John indeed baptized with water; but ye shall be baptized with the Holy Ghost. (17) Forasmuch then as God gave them the like gift as he did unto us, who believed

103

on the Lord Jesus Christ; what was I, that I could withstand God? (18) When they heard these things, they held their peace, and glorified God, saying, Then hath God also to the Gentiles granted repentance unto life" (Acts 11:15-18).

"(7) And when there had been much disputing, Peter rose up, and said unto them, Men and brethren, ye know how that a good while ago God made choice among us, that the Gentiles by my mouth should hear the word of the gospel, and believe. (8) And God, which knoweth the hearts, bare them witness, giving them the Holy Ghost, even as he did unto us; (9) And put no difference between us and them, purifying their hearts by faith...(11) But we believe that through the grace of the Lord Jesus Christ we shall be saved, even as they"
(Acts 15:7-9, 11).

The New Testament salvation experience of Cornelius and other Gentiles (in Acts 10:44-48, 11:15-18, and 15:7-11) included:
1. Hearing the word of God preached by Peter (Acts 10:44; 15:7).
2. Believing what Peter preached (Acts 11:17; 15:7).
3. Receiving the gift of the Holy Ghost with the initial evidence of speaking in tongues (Acts 10:45-47). Peter said that these Gentiles received the Holy Ghost "as well as we" (Acts 10:47, KJV) or "just as we have" (Acts 10:47, NKJV). Peter also said that God gave them the Holy Ghost: *"as on us at the beginning" (Acts 11:15)*, and *"even as he did unto us" (Acts 15:8)*. The Gentiles received the gift of the Holy Ghost just like Peter and others did on the Day of Pentecost in Acts chapter 2, speaking in other tongues (Acts 2:4-11, 33).
4. Being baptized in water "in the name of the Lord" (Acts 10:48, KJV) or "in the name of Jesus Christ" (Acts 10:48, NIV).
5. The grace of God (Acts 15:11) and the faith of each individual for their heart to be purified (Acts 15:9).
6. God granting them "repentance unto life" (Acts 11:18).

Even though the salvation experience of Cornelius and other Gentiles included both "speaking in tongues" when they received the Holy Ghost (Acts 10:45-47), and being baptized in water (Acts 10:48), neither of these details were mentioned in Acts 11:15-18 and Acts 15:7-11.

Paul to "Disciples of John the Baptist" in Ephesus (Acts 19:1-7)

"(1) And it came to pass, that, while Apollos was at Corinth, Paul having passed through the upper coasts came to Ephesus: and finding certain disciples, (2) He said unto them, Have ye received the Holy Ghost since ye believed? And they said unto him, We have not so much as heard whether there be any Holy Ghost. (3) And he said unto them, Unto what then were ye baptized? And they said, Unto John's baptism. (4) Then said Paul, John verily baptized with the baptism of repentance, saying unto the people, that they should believe on him which should come after him, that is, on Christ Jesus. (5) When they heard this, they were baptized in the name of the Lord Jesus. (6) And when Paul had laid his hands upon them, the Holy Ghost came on them; and they spake with tongues, and prophesied. (7) And all the men were about twelve" (Acts 19:1-7).

Acts 19:1-2: This was around twenty-two years after the day of Pentecost in Acts 2 (refer to "Chronology of Book of Acts & Life of Paul" on page 60). Paul met certain disciples of John the Baptist in Ephesus. Paul asked these disciples *"Did you receive the Holy Spirit when you believed?" (Acts 19:2, NKJV)*. These disciples of John the Baptist in Ephesus said *"We have not so much heard whether there be any Holy Ghost" (Acts 19:2)*. Even though John the Baptist preached that the one coming after him, Jesus Christ, would baptize believers with the Holy Ghost (Matthew 3:11), apparently these disciples had never heard about anyone receiving this New Testament experience.

Acts 19:3-4: Since these people never heard of someone receiving the Holy Ghost, Paul asked them how they had been baptized. They said that they had been baptized by John the Baptist. Paul explained that John the Baptist baptized with a baptism of repentance, saying that they should believe on the one coming after him, Christ Jesus.

Acts 19:5-7: Paul rebaptized these people in the name of the Lord Jesus. When Paul laid his hands upon them, these twelve men received the gift of the Holy Ghost, and *"they spake with tongues, and prophesied" (Acts 19:6)*.

Ananias to Paul
(Acts 9:1-18; 22:1-16)

Ananias came to Paul so that he could receive his sight and *"be filled with the Holy Ghost" (Acts 9:17).* Ananias told Paul, *"And now why tarriest thou? Arise, and be baptized, and wash away thy sins, calling on the name of the Lord" (Acts 22:16).* Paul *"was baptized" (Acts 9:18).* Paul later wrote, *"I thank my God, I speak with tongues more than ye all" (1 Corinthians 14:18).*

Paul's Total Commitment to God

Paul surrendered his will to God's will. Paul must have thoroughly repented after God blinded him on the road to Damascus. Paul realized the great price that Jesus Christ paid for his salvation on a cross at Calvary (Luke 23:33; Romans 5:8; 2 Corinthians 5:14-15). Paul said that he was a debtor to others (Romans 1:14). Paul was undoubtedly very thankful to His great God and Savior for numerous reasons, including:

- Extending mercy to him, a chief-sinner who ignorantly persecuted God's blood-brought bride (1 Timothy 1:12-15).
- Opening his eyes to the precious truth of the gospel (Acts 26:18; Ephesians 3:3-6).
- Allowing him the privilege and honor to be involved in God's work on earth (1 Thessalonians 2:4; Ephesians 3:7-8).

Paul described the "Spirit of Christ" (Romans 8:9-11) and God working in us in various ways:

> *"The riches of the glory...which is Christ in you, the hope of glory" (Colossians 1:27)*
>
> *"His working, which worketh in me mightily" (Colossians 1:29)*
>
> *"To be strengthened with might by his Spirit in the inner man" (Ephesians 3:16)*
>
> *"The power that worketh in us" (Ephesians 3:20)*
>
> *"We have this treasure in earthen vessels" (2 Corinthians 4:7).*

The words "earthen vessels" (2 Corinthians 4:7, KJV) are translated as "jars of clay" (NIV).

The Age of Accountability

The Bible is written for individuals that are able to believe and repent. An innocent infant does not realize or understand their sinful nature (and need of salvation) until they mature and reach "the age of accountability." Individuals that are mentally incapable of understanding the plan of salvation may never reach "the age of accountability." David said regarding his infant son that died: *"I shall go to him, but he shall not return to me" (2 Samuel 12:23)*. As stated by Abraham, *"Shall not the Judge of all the earth do right?" (Genesis 18:25)*. We put innocent infants and mentally-incapable individuals in the hands of our loving and merciful God.

Final Thoughts on New Testament Salvation

The Bible teaches that "being baptized in water" and "receiving the Holy Ghost" are separate experiences. A person can receive the Holy Ghost *before* (as in Acts 10:44-48) or *after* (as in Acts 8:12-17) they have been baptized in water.

Peter, Paul, Philip, and Ananias all preached the same New Testament plan of salvation message (Acts 2:38). Philip was *"full of the Holy Ghost" (Acts 6:3)*, chosen by the twelve apostles (Acts 6:2-7), and still connected to the apostles in Acts chapter 8. Philip's revival meetings in Samaria did not end when these Samaritans believed and were baptized in the name of Jesus. Why? They had *not yet* received the Holy Ghost (Acts 8:16). Philip did not leave Samaria (Acts 8:26) until *after* the Samaritans received the Holy Ghost with some external sign given (Acts 8:17-19). The external sign given to the Samaritans was undoubtedly *speaking in other tongues*, since that is the sign given throughout the book of Acts (Acts 2:4-11, 33; 10:44-47; 19:6-7).

Jesus shed his blood for the sins of the whole world (1 John 2:2), but why are only few saved (Matthew 7:13-14)? Because not everyone obeys the New Testament plan of salvation preached by Peter (and the other apostles) in the book of Acts (1 Peter 1:22-25; Galatians 1:6-9; 2 Thessalonians 1:7-10).

11 - <u>Speaking in Tongues</u>

<u>God's Choice of Tongues</u>

Our God-given ability to intelligently communicate to God and others, through our speech, makes us a higher order of creation than any other living creature. Only humans (not animals or any other living creatures) were created with the ability to have a relationship with God through communication. How do we communicate with God? Through our *speech*. We are able to understand when God talks or communicates with us with His *"still small voice" (1 Kings 19:12)* or impressions that He gives to us. David stated, *"Who can understand his errors? Cleanse thou me from secret faults" (Psalm 19:12).* Paul said that he was striving *"to have always a conscience void of offense toward God, and toward men" (Acts 24:16).* God communicates with us and we can express our thoughts, feelings, and ideas to God. We can cast all of our cares upon God, for He cares for us (1 Peter 5:7). We can bring all of our prayer requests before God's throne of grace (Hebrews 4:16), which is communication to God with our speech.

When someone receives the gift of the Holy Ghost with the initial outward evidence of *speaking in other tongues,* this refers to *speaking in a language unknown to them*, as the Spirit of God gives them utterance. I do not claim to know why God choose speaking in tongues as the initial evidence of receiving the gift of the Holy Ghost (Acts 2:4-11, 33; 10:45-46; 19:6).

God has His own purpose in whatever He does (Ephesians 1:11; Acts 4:28). God's thoughts and ways are higher than our thoughts and ways (Isaiah 55:8-9). God's ways are past finding out (Romans 11:33). "For who hath known the mind of the Lord? Or who hath been his counsellor?" (Romans 11:34). Here are some thoughts to consider. **Speaking in tongues is**:

1. ***Consistent external evidence.*** Every one receives the Holy Ghost with the same external outward sign. Jesus said that when someone is "born of the Spirit" (John 3:8), which refers to when someone receives the Holy Ghost, they will *hear a sound* (John 3:8). How do I know the wind is blowing? I hear the rustling of the leaves. What do we hear when a new born

baby breathes its first breath? A *sound*. Speaking in tongues is an outward sign that each person and others can both *see* and *hear*. Peter said *"having received of the Father the promise of the Holy Ghost, he hath shed forth this, which ye now see and hear" (Acts 2:33)*. The words "he hath shed forth this" (Acts 2:33, KJV) are translated as "He poured out this" (NKJV). How do I know that someone has been born of the Spirit (or received the gift of the Holy Ghost)? They will always have the same initial evidence of speaking in tongues as the Spirit of God gives them utterance. This "consistent" sign will help each individual and others "to know" that they received the gift of the Holy Ghost.

2. ***An outward sign of the Holy Ghost dwelling in us.*** Every individual will receive the Holy Ghost when they are seeking God in some way, such as praying to God or worshipping God. In John 7:37-39, Jesus said that when someone receives the Holy Ghost, *"Rivers of living water shall flow out of their "heart" (John 7:38, NKJV)* or "innermost being" (John 7:38, AMPCE). Jesus said: *"Out of the abundance of the heart, the mouth speaketh" (Matthew 12:34)*, and *"Those things which proceed out of the mouth come forth from the heart" (Matthew 15:18)*. When the Spirit of God sets up a permanent residence in us (1 Corinthians 3:16-17; 2 Corinthians 6:16), and writes His laws in our heart (2 Corinthians 3:3; Hebrews 8:10; 10:16), then as we speak in tongues, it is an outward sign of the Holy Ghost dwelling (living) in us (Romans 8:11; 2 Timothy 1:14).

3. ***An outward sign of being completely yielded to God.*** The tongue is the most unruly member of the body that no man can tame (James 3:8). Only God can tame the tongue. When God fills us with His Spirit and we *"speak with tongues, and magnify God" (Acts 10:46)*, it is a sign that all of the members of our body, including our tongue, have yielded to God (James 3:2-10).

110

Use of Tongues in God's New Testament Church

When referring to the gift of the Holy Ghost, the Greek word for "gift" is *dorea* (Acts 2:38; 8:20; 10:45; 11:17). When referring to any of the nine gifts of the Spirit (1 Corinthians 12:4-11, 28-31), including "different kinds of tongues" (1 Corinthians 12:10, NKJV), the Greek word for "gift" is *charisma*. Anyone that has received the "gift" (Greek: *dorea*) of the Holy Ghost and is a member of God's New Testament Church, can also be used by God in any of the nine spiritual "gifts" (plural of Greek: *charisma*) mentioned in 1 Corinthians 12:8-10:

> *"(4) Now there are diversities of gifts* [plural of Greek *charisma*], *but the same Spirit. (5) And there are differences of administrations, but the same Lord. (6) And there are diversities of operations, but it is the same God which worketh all in all. (7) But the manifestation of the Spirit is given to every man to profit withal. (8) For to one is given by the Spirit the word of wisdom; to another the word of knowledge by the same Spirit; (9) To another faith by the same Spirit; to another the gifts of healing by the same Spirit; (10) To another the working of miracles; to another prophecy; to another discerning of spirits; to another divers kinds of tongues; to another the interpretation of tongues: (11) But all these worketh that one and the selfsame Spirit, dividing to every man severally as he will" (1 Corinthians 12:4-11).*

Whenever God chooses to work through His church members with one or more of His nine spiritual gifts, it is for the "profit of all" (1 Corinthians 12:7, NKJV). This includes any of the three vocal gifts mentioned in 1 Corinthians 12:10: (a) Prophecy, (b) "Divers" (KJV) or "different" (NKJV) kinds of tongues, and (c) The interpretation of tongues.

There is a difference between the "gift" (Greek: *dorea*) of the Holy Ghost and the spiritual "gift" (Greek: *charisma*) of different kinds of tongues. Paul wrote the epistle of 1 Corinthians to individuals that had already received the "gift" (Greek: *dorea*) of the Holy Ghost.

Paul explains that all people that have received the "gift" (Greek: *dorea*) of the Holy Ghost, *do not* have the "gift" (Greek: *charisma*) of different kinds of tongues:

> *"(28) And God hath set some in the church, first apostles, secondarily prophets, thirdly teachers, after that miracles, then gifts of healings, helps, governments, diversities of tongues. (29) Are all apostles? are all prophets? are all teachers? are all workers of miracles? (30) Have all the gifts of healing? do all speak with tongues? do all interpret? (31) But covet earnestly the best gifts [plural of Greek charisma]: and yet shew I unto you a more excellent way" (1 Corinthians 12:28-31).*

In 1 Corinthians 12:28-30, Paul says that *some* have the "gift" (Greek: *charisma*) of "diversities" (KJV) or "varieties" (NKJV) of tongues. In 1 Corinthians 12:30, Paul asks "Do all speak with tongues?" This question is referring to the "gift" (Greek: *charisma*) of different kinds of tongues, which is one of the nine "gifts" (plural of Greek *charisma*) of the Spirit mentioned in 1 Corinthians 12. The answer to all questions in 1 Corinthians 12:29-30 is *"No."*

Speaking in tongues refers to someone speaking in *a language unknown to them* when initially receiving the gift of the Holy Ghost, praying to God, worshipping God, or giving a divine message (usually during a church gathering) to others. The Bible mentions "tongues of men and of angels" (1 Corinthians 13:1) and "an unknown tongue" (1 Corinthians 14:2). Normally, no one understands what they are saying, when they:

1. **Speak in an unknown tongue.** *"For he that speaketh in an unknown tongue speaketh not unto men, but unto God: for no man understandeth him; howbeit in the spirit he speaketh mysteries" (1 Corinthians 14:2).*
2. **"Pray in an unknown tongue" (or "pray with the spirit") or "sing with the spirit."** *"For if I pray in an unknown tongue, my spirit prayeth, but my understanding is unfruitful. What is it then? I will pray with the spirit, and I will pray with the understanding also: I will sing with the spirit, and I will sing with the understanding also" (1 Corinthians 14:14-15).*

3. **"Bless with the spirit."** *"Else when thou shalt bless with the spirit, how shall he that occupieth the room of the unlearned say Amen at thy giving of thanks, seeing he understandeth not what thou sayest? For thou verily givest thanks well, but the other is not edified" (1 Corinthians 14:16-17).*

Speaking in Tongues by Members of God's Church (Acts 20:28) or Christ's Body (Romans 12:4-5; 1 Corinthians 12:12-27)	
Gift	**Purpose**
The "gift" (Greek: *dorea*) of the Holy Ghost	The initial evidence of receiving the gift of the Holy Ghost (Acts 2:4-11, 33; 10:44-47; 19:6-7). There were probably at least 120 people (Acts 1:15) in Acts chapter 2, Cornelius and his household in Acts chapter 10, and twelve men in Acts 19:7. I attended a Holy Ghost Crusade preached by Rev. Billy Cole at the US Cellular Building in Milwaukee, WI. During this service, over 100 people received the Holy Ghost with the initial sign of speaking in tongues.
The spiritual "gift" (Greek: *charisma*) of different kinds of tongues	For personal edification during prayer or worship to God. *"He that speaketh in an unknown tongue edifieth himself" (1 Corinthians 14:4).* Paul said, *"I thank my God, I speak with tongues more than ye all" (1 Corinthians 14:18).* Paul understood the value of speaking in tongues while worshipping God or praying.
	For edification of the church assembly when it is interpreted during a public gathering (1 Corinthians chapter 14).
Note: There is no need for an interpreter when someone receives the "gift" (Greek: *dorea*) of the Holy Ghost or speaks in unknown tongues for personal edification.	

113

Personal Prayer to God with the Help of God's Spirit

Praying "in the Spirit" (Ephesians 6:18) or "in the Holy Ghost" (Jude 20) builds up ourselves. Praying "in the Spirit" may refer to having Spirit-led prayer in your known language (for example, English) or praying in an unknown tongue:

> *"Praying always with all prayer and supplication in the Spirit, and watching thereunto with all perseverance and supplication for all saints" (Ephesians 6:18).*

> *"But ye, beloved, building up yourselves on your most holy faith, praying in the Holy Ghost" (Jude 20).*

According to Romans 8:26-27, the Holy Spirit in us will help our "infirmities" (Romans 8:26, KJV) or "weaknesses" (NKJV) as we pray "according to the will of God" during intercessory prayer for ourselves or others:

> *"(26) Likewise the Spirit also helpeth our infirmities: for we know not what we should pray for as we ought: but the Spirit itself maketh intercession for us with groanings which cannot be uttered. (27) And he that searcheth the hearts knoweth what is the mind of the Spirit, because he maketh intercession for the saints according to the will of God" (Romans 8:26-27).*

This may include praying in an unknown tongue, *"for we know not what we should pray for as we ought" (Romans 8:26).* This deep dimension of prayer includes "groanings which cannot be uttered" (Romans 8:26, KJV) or "groans that words cannot express" (Romans 8:26, NIV).

Proper Regulation of the Vocal Spiritual Gifts During a Church Gathering

Paul mentions the following three vocal spiritual gifts in 1 Corinthians 12:10: (a) Prophecy, (b) Different kinds of tongues, and (c) The interpretation of tongues. Our heart must be right and our motives must be pure whenever God chooses to work through us with one of His spiritual gifts, which is for the benefit of the entire body of Christ (1 Corinthians 12:7, 12-31). Paul explains that whenever any spiritual gifts mentioned in 1 Corinthians 12:8-10 are operated by God through one of His members, the use of these gifts must be done with love (1 Corinthians 13:1-13). Parts of 1 Corinthians chapter 14 explain that when the members of the church come together and God works through someone to give a public message in tongues, it will be of no value to the church (or others) unless someone gives an interpretation of the message:

"(1) Follow after charity, and desire spiritual gifts, but rather that ye may prophesy. (2) For he that speaketh in an unknown tongue speaketh not unto men, but unto God: for no man understandeth him; howbeit in the spirit he speaketh mysteries. (3) But he that prophesieth speaketh unto men to edification, and exhortation, and comfort. (4) He that speaketh in an unknown tongue edifieth himself; but he that prophesieth edifieth the church. (5) I would that ye all spake with tongues, but rather that ye prophesied: for greater is he that prophesieth than he that speaketh with tongues, except he interpret, that the church may receive edifying" (1 Corinthians 14:1-5).

Verse 1: The words "but rather that ye may prophesy" (KJV) are translated as "especially the gift of prophecy" (NIV). To "prophesy" (or the gift of prophecy) refers to anointed speech to others in their known language.

Verses 3-4: "He that prophesieth" (anointed speech to others in their known language) edifies the church. These words to others are for: (a) "Edification" (KJV) or "strengthening" (NIV), (b) "Exhortation" (KJV) or "encouragement" (NIV), and (c) Comfort.

Verse 5: In a church gathering, if someone gives a message in an unknown tongue with an interpretation, it has the same value as "he that prophesieth" (gives a message in their known language).

115

"(12) Even so ye, forasmuch as ye are zealous of spiritual gifts, seek that ye may excel to the edifying of the church. (13) Wherefore let him that speaketh in an unknown tongue pray that he may interpret...(18) I thank my God, I speak with tongues more than ye all: (19) Yet in the church I had rather speak five words with my understanding, that by my voice I might teach others also, than ten thousand words in an unknown tongue"...(23) If therefore the whole church be come together into one place, and all speak with tongues, and there come in those that are unlearned, or unbelievers, will they not say that ye are mad?...(26) How is it then, brethren? when ye come together, every one of you hath a psalm, hath a doctrine, hath a tongue, hath a revelation, hath an interpretation. Let all things be done unto edifying. (27) If any man speak in an unknown tongue, let it be by two, or at the most by three, and that by course; and let one interpret. (28) But if there be no interpreter, let him keep silence in the church; and let him speak to himself, and to God"
(1 Corinthians 14:12-13, 18-19, 23, 26-28).

Whenever someone gives a message in an unknown tongue during a church gathering:

Verses 12-13: The church should pray for an interpretation, so that the church is edified.

Verse 19: The church is not edified if there is no interpretation.

Verse 23: The unlearned or unbelievers will think you are "mad" (KJV) or "out of your mind" (NKJV) if there is no interpretation.

Verses 26-27: Two or at the most three should speak, "that by course" (KJV) or "one at a time" (NIV), and let one interpret.

Verse 28: If there is no interpreter, let him keep "silence" (KJV) or "silent" (NKJV) in the church, and let him speak to himself and to God. Why? Because the church will not be edified unless someone interprets the message into their known language.

I have been in church services where there was a temporary silence, followed by someone used in "the gift of prophecy" (1 Corinthians 14:1, NIV) to give an audible message in English to the church. I have also been in church services where there was: (a) A brief pause, followed by someone giving a divine message in an unknown tongue, and then (b) Another short period of silence, while everyone prayed quietly, and then someone else (or the same individual) gave an English interpretation of the "unknown tongue" message.

Final Thoughts on Speaking in Tongues

Sometimes people misunderstand the difference between receiving the "gift" (Greek: *dorea*) of the Holy Ghost with the initial evidence of speaking in tongues and the spiritual "gift" (Greek: *charisma*) of *different kinds of tongues* mentioned in 1 Corinthians chapter 12. I have heard people say: "I received the gift of the Holy Ghost, but I never spoke in tongues because I don't have the gift of tongues." I have tried to explain that there is a difference between the "gift" (Greek: *dorea*) of the Holy Ghost and the spiritual "gift" (Greek: *charisma*) of different kinds of tongues. Every one that receives the "gift" (Greek: *dorea*) of the Holy Ghost (John 3:8; 7:37-39) will speak in tongues as the initial outward sign. After being filled with the Holy Ghost, they may also speak in tongues while worshipping God or praying. However, not everybody that receives the "gift" (Greek: *dorea*) of the Holy Ghost is used by God in the public spiritual "gift" (Greek: *charisma*) of different kinds of tongues.

I have never given a message in an unknown tongue during a church service. However, I spoke in tongues when I initially received the Holy Ghost. I also normally speak in tongues during my daily prayer time, during pre-service church prayer, when I am worshipping God, or when I am praying for others. I do not try to speak in tongues, but as I am praying in English, the Spirit of God will periodically intercede and I will "pray in an unknown tongue" (1 Corinthians 14:14). While "praying in an unknown tongue," I will not understand what I am praying (1 Corinthians 14:2, 14-15). I will go back and forth between praying in an unknown tongue and praying in English.

Paul said that tongues "shall cease" (1 Corinthians 13:8) when God's Church has been "caught up" to be with Jesus Christ forever in His eternal kingdom (1 Corinthians 13:10, 12; 1 Thessalonians 4:13-18; Revelation 19:7-9). But until then, we are to *"forbid not to speak in tongues" (1 Corinthians 14:39).*

12 - <u>The Fire of the Holy Ghost</u>

John the Baptist said that Jesus would baptize us with the Holy Ghost and with *fire* (Matthew 3:11; Luke 3:16). When I received the baptism of the Holy Ghost, there was an intense *fire* that burned in my inner man. It was something that I had never experienced before:

The "FIRE of God" was included in:	Scriptures
God's call to Moses (Exodus 3:1-6)	*"And the angel of the LORD appeared unto him in a flame of fire out of the midst of a bush: and he looked, and, behold, the bush burned with fire, and the bush was not consumed" (Exodus 3:2).*
God's presence at night (Exodus 13:21-22; 40:38; Numbers 9:15-23)	God led the nation of Israel out of Egypt to the land of Canaan: *"By day in a pillar of a cloud, to lead them the way; and by night in a pillar of fire, to give them light" (Exodus 13:21).*
The giving of the Law to Moses on Mount Sinai (Exodus 24:16-18)	God descended upon Mount Sinai in fire (Exodus 19:18) and *"the sight of the glory of the LORD was like devouring fire on the top of the mount" (Exodus 24:17).*
The tabernacle in the wilderness and temple in Jerusalem	God *sent fire to consume* the animal sacrifices in the brazen altars of the tabernacle (Leviticus 9:24) and temple (2 Chronicles 7:1-3).
Isaiah's vision of God and the angels around His throne (Isaiah 6:1-8)	An angel took a *burning fiery coal* from the altar in heaven and touched Isaiah (Isaiah 6:6-7).

The "FIRE of God" was included in:	Scriptures
Ezekiel's vision of God and the angels below His throne (Ezekiel 1:1-28)	Ezekiel saw what appeared to be a throne with a man on it, high above four fiery "living creatures" (KJV) or "living creatures [or cherubim]" (Ezekiel 1:5, AMPCE) in Ezekiel 1:1-28. *"Also from the appearance of His waist and upward I saw, as it were, the color of amber with the appearance of fire all around within it; and from the appearance of His waist and downward I saw, as it were, the appearance of fire with brightness all around" (Ezekiel 1:27, NKJV).*
Daniel's vision of God on His throne (Daniel 7:9-10)	*"The Ancient of days did sit, whose garment was white as snow, and the hair of his head like the pure wool: his throne was like the fiery flame, and his wheels as burning fire. A fiery stream issued and came forth from before him" (Daniel 7:9-10).*
John's vision of Jesus and God's throne in heaven (Revelation 1:10-20; 4:2, 5; 7:17)	John saw Jesus in the middle of seven golden candlesticks (Revelation 1:12-13) and said: *"His head and his hairs were white like wool, as white as snow; and his eyes were as a flame of fire; And his feet like unto fine brass, as if they burned in a furnace; and his voice as the sound of many waters" (Revelation 1:14-15).* *"A throne was set in heaven, and one sat on the throne...and there were seven lamps of fire burning before the throne" (Revelation 4:2, 5).* *"The Lamb which is in the midst of the throne" (Revelation 7:17).*

The *fire* that comes with the Holy Ghost is very similar to what happened to the prophet Isaiah in chapter 6 of the book of Isaiah:

"(1) In the year that king Uzziah died I saw also the Lord sitting upon a throne, high and lifted up, and his train filled the temple. (2) Above it stood the seraphims: each one had six wings; with twain he covered his face, and with twain he covered his feet, and with twain he did fly. (3) And one cried unto another, and said, Holy, holy, holy, is the LORD of hosts: the whole earth is full of his glory. (4) And the posts of the door moved at the voice of him that cried, and the house was filled with smoke. (5) Then said I, Woe is me! for I am undone; because I am a man of unclean lips, and I dwell in the midst of a people of unclean lips: for mine eyes have seen the King, the LORD of hosts. (6) Then flew one of the seraphims unto me, having a live coal in his hand, which he had taken with the tongs from off the altar: (7) And he laid it upon my mouth, and said, Lo, this hath touched thy lips; and thine iniquity is taken away, and thy sin purged. (8) Also I heard the voice of the Lord, saying, Whom shall I send, and who will go for us? Then said I, Here am I; send me" (Isaiah 6:1-8).

After Isaiah saw a vision of the Holy One of Israel on His throne, he realized how unclean that he was and he said "Woe is me!" (Isaiah 6:5). Not only did the *fire* of God from heaven take away Isaiah's sin (Isaiah 6:6-7), but it also put a *fire* in him that made him want to be involved in the work of God (Isaiah 6:8). After that day, Isaiah was never the same!

One day, God filled me with the Holy Ghost, and I have never been the same! Jesus touched my inner man, got ahold of my heart, and totally changed everything about me. Something so holy, pure, and clean touched me. Similar to Isaiah, the *fire* of God from heaven not only cleansed and purified me, but also put a deep desire in me to reach out to others with this precious truth.

Just like the prophet Isaiah, we are like cold men coming to the *fire* of God to be warmed. We cannot warm ourselves or cleanse ourselves from our own sins, but instead, we need God's Spirit to warm us, cleanse us, and keep us clean. When we get in the presence of God, we see ourselves the way that we really are. We need the *fire* of God's Spirit to search our hearts and to keep our thoughts and motives pure. The more that I get in the presence of God, the more that I want to get in the presence of God again and again. God's Spirit renews and transforms our minds (Romans 12:2; Ephesians 4:23), helping us to maintain a right perspective, a right way to look at things, a right way to view all the things that are going on in our lives.

Prior to my conversion experience, my inner man felt very cold and empty. *After my conversion experience*, my inner man felt "on-fire" and full. There was a *fire* burning within me for others to receive what I had received from God. The Spirit of Jesus Christ living inside of me really dealt with me to tell others about my conversion experience and invite them to church. The feeling of excitement and enthusiasm in my innermost being cannot really be properly expressed in words.

Prior to my conversion experience, I sat quietly in the pew during the worship service. *After my conversion experience*, I often got out into the aisle and danced, or jumped up and down, or ran around the church during the worship service. I often clapped my hands and shouted unto God. It was a totally different feeling after God filled me with the Holy Ghost. There was a deep desire in me to get in the flow of whatever God was doing during a particular service. During worship service, it was another opportunity for me to express my heartfelt thanks, praise, and worship to the God that had spared my soul. I wanted to lift up my hands and thank God for calling me out of darkness into His marvelous light. There were many of us that wanted to celebrate what God had done in our lives. We wanted to touch God and wanted God to touch us and move in our hearts. We wanted the fire of God to fall and refresh us, renew us, and empower us to do His will.

There was usually an altar call at the end of every church service. Most people would go to the altar and pray alone or with someone else. I remember staying at the church for hours after a Sunday night church service had ended and everybody had gone home. I would go in one of the rooms near the sanctuary and pray for a long time. Why? I had never felt or experienced the presence of God in such an awesome and powerful way.

I could not get enough of church. I would pray and study the Bible for many hours each day. There was a deep desire in me to know more about God and what He had done in my life. I would invite many people to church. There was a deep compassion in me for others to experience what God had blessed me to receive.

God sent fire from heaven to both start the fire and consume the animal sacrifice in the brazen altars of the tabernacle (Leviticus 9:24) and temple (2 Chronicles 7:1-3). However, then it was the responsibility of the priests to maintain the fire that God sent from heaven. The fire on the brazen altar was to *never go out* (Leviticus 6:9, 12-13). So it is in our lives. We need the *fire* of God's Spirit to keep our lights burning (Luke 12:35; Matthew 25:1-10), and be a light to others (Matthew 5:14-16; Philippians 2:15). Every day, we need to touch God and we need God to touch us.

Sometimes God will visit us and bless us with His presence. It is difficult to explain what you feel when you sit in your chair and you are suddenly overwhelmed by the presence of God. The presence of God causes you to begin weeping, praying, and worshipping God.

The gift of the Holy Ghost is so awesome and great that no words can adequately describe it. The gift of the Holy Ghost is the greatest gift and the most glorious experience available to every individual in this world. After I received it, I wanted to tell everyone about this wonderful gift.

13 - <u>The Fruit of the Spirit</u>

Someone that has received the gift of the Holy Ghost will experience the nine different fruit of the Spirit mentioned by Paul in the book of Galatians: *"The fruit of the Spirit is love, joy, peace, longsuffering, gentleness, goodness, faith, Meekness, temperance" (Galatians 5:22-23).*

There is simply no way to properly describe what it feels like to have the Spirit of Jesus Christ residing inside of you. I was in *awe* when I received the gift of the Holy Ghost, and have been in *awe* ever since. Jesus walks with me and talks with me. Jesus is truly such a dear personal friend to me at all times and in all places. It is something far bigger and greater than anything else that I have experienced in this life.

<u>Love</u>

Paul said, *"To know the love of Christ, which passeth knowledge" (Ephesians 3:19).*

"The love of Christ" that you feel, not only from God, but also for others is indescribable. I had never experienced such an intense heartfelt love for God and others. I had never before felt such a deep feeling of compassion for someone that was a complete stranger to me.

I had never experienced what it meant to *"weep between the porch and the altar" (Joel 2:17)* while asking God to spare others. I would weep for long periods of time for people that were "lost" and not ready to meet God.

Sometimes I would get angry at those that would try to hinder me in some way from serving the God that I so greatly desired to please. But then, I would have a prayer meeting with Jesus. During my prayer meeting, God would replace my anger for them with a deep compassion for the lost condition of their soul. Instead of being angry at them, I actually felt sorry for them because they were so spiritually blind to what I had received from God.

Joy

Peter said that because of our salvation experience, we:
"Rejoice with joy unspeakable and full of glory" (1 Peter 1:8) or
"Are filled with an inexpressible and glorious joy"
(1 Peter 1:8; NIV).

When I received the Holy Ghost, there was such an indescribable feeling of joy in me. It made me want to sing and shout "Hallelujah!" It made me want to clap my hands, dance, and "leap for joy" (Luke 6:23).

I remember singing the chorus of the song Joy Unspeakable by Barney Elliot Warren: "It is joy unspeakable and full of glory, Full of glory, full of glory; It is joy unspeakable and full of glory, Oh, the half has never yet been told."

Peter also said:

> *"Beloved, think it not strange concerning the fiery trial which is to try you, as though some strange thing happened unto you: But rejoice, inasmuch as ye are partakers of Christ's sufferings; that, when his glory shall be revealed, ye may be glad also with exceeding joy" (1 Peter 4:12-13).*

Jesus said:

> *"Rejoice, because your names are written in heaven" (Luke 10:20)*
>
> *"In the world ye shall have tribulation: but be of good cheer; I have overcome the world." (John 16:33).*

After three missionary journeys, Paul said:

> *"And now, behold, I go bound in the spirit unto Jerusalem, not knowing the things that shall befall me there: Save that the Holy Ghost witnesseth in every city, saying that bonds and afflictions abide me. But none of these things move me, neither count I my life dear unto myself, so that I might finish my course **with joy**, and the ministry, which I have received of the Lord Jesus, to testify the gospel of the grace of God" (Acts 20:22-24).*

When Paul went to Jerusalem, a group of Jews tried to kill him, but some Roman soldiers rescued Paul (Acts 21:27-40). Paul was allowed to give his testimony to some Jews (Acts 21:40-22:21) and appeared the next day before the Jewish Sanhedrin (Acts 23:1-10). In both instances where Paul tried to reach out to some Jews with his testimony, he was greatly opposed (Acts 22:22-23; 23:10). After this, Jesus spoke to Paul in the night and told him:

"Be of good cheer, Paul: for as thou hast testified of me in Jerusalem, so must thou bear witness also at Rome" (Acts 23:11).

After Paul was taken by night to Caesarea and appeared before the Roman governor Felix and some Jewish leaders, Paul said: *"I do the more cheerfully answer for myself" (Acts 24:10).* After Paul was imprisoned in Caesarea for two years (Acts 24:27), he appeared before king Agrippa and said: *"I think myself happy, king Agrippa" (Acts 26:2).* After Paul "appealed unto Caesar" (Acts 26:32), he was taken to Rome on a ship as a prisoner and they encountered a great storm and did not eat any food for two weeks (Acts 27:1-22, 33-35). Paul said to those on the ship with him:

"And now I exhort you to be of good cheer: for there shall be no loss of any man's life among you, but of the ship. For there stood by me this night the angel of God, whose I am, and whom I serve, Saying, Fear not, Paul; thou must be brought before Caesar: and, lo, God hath given thee all them that sail with thee. Wherefore, sirs, be of good cheer: for I believe God, that it shall be even as it was told me." (Acts 27:22-25).

Paul had learned the importance of rejoicing in God, no matter what came his way! Paul told the Philippians, when he wrote a letter to them during his first Roman imprisonment, *"Rejoice in the Lord" (Philippians 3:1),* and *"Rejoice in the Lord always. Again I will say, rejoice!" (Philippians 4:4; NKJV).*

Peace

Paul wrote about, *"The peace of God, which passeth all understanding" (Philippians 4:7).*

After receiving the Holy Ghost, there was an inner peace between God and me that I had never experienced before. It was an indescribable feeling of a perfect peace or calmness in my innermost being. Since receiving the Holy Ghost, I have tried to let

Jesus Christ, the Prince of Peace (Isaiah 9:6), rule and reign in my heart (Colossians 3:15). There have been times, while going through a storm or trial, when I have felt such a wonderful peace of God in my inner man.

Victory Through Jesus over Our Sinful Nature

After we are born-again and receive the gift of the Holy Ghost, there will still be a continual struggle between our born-again "new man" (Ephesians 4:24; Colossians 3:10) and our "old man" (Ephesians 4:22; Colossians 3:9) or *sinful nature* that we were born with (Ephesians 2:3). In order to continually bear the "Fruit of the Spirit" (Galatians 5:22-23), we will have to contend with our sinful nature or "flesh" until the day that we die. Paul said:

> *"For I know that in me (that is, in my flesh,) dwelleth no good thing" (Romans 7:18).*

> *"When I would do good, evil is present with me" (Romans 7:21).*

> *"Walk in the Spirit and you shall not fulfill the lust of the flesh" (Galatians 5:16).*

> *"They that are Christ's have crucified the flesh with the affections and lusts" (Galatians 5:24).*

Paul had to submit his human will to the will of God every day. Paul said:

> *"I am crucified with Christ: nevertheless I live; yet not I, but Christ liveth in me: and the life which I now live in the flesh I live by the faith of the Son of God, who loved me, and gave himself for me" (Galatians 2:20).*

> *"I die daily" (1 Corinthians 15:31).*

Paul let us know that the key to living a victorious life in Jesus Christ is to have the Spirit of God in us ruling and reigning over our sinful flesh (Romans 8:1-13) or "old man" (Romans 6:6).

14 - <u>A Victorious Life</u>

<u>Victory in Our Spiritual Battle</u>

The Bible lets us know that we are all involved in a spiritual battle:

> *"For though we walk in the flesh, we do not war after the flesh: (For the weapons of our warfare are not carnal, but mighty through God to the pulling down of strong holds;) Casting down imaginations, and every high thing that exalteth itself against the knowledge of God, and bringing into captivity every thought to the obedience of Christ"*
> *(2 Corinthians 10:3-5).*

> *"Submit yourselves therefore to God. Resist the devil, and he will flee from you" (James 4:7).*

> *"Be sober, be vigilant; because your adversary the devil, as a roaring lion, walketh about, seeking whom he may devour"*
> *(1 Peter 5:8).*

We desperately need to meet regularly (Hebrews 10:25) with people of "like precious faith" (2 Peter 1:1) and submit ourselves to a godly pastor (Hebrews 13:17) to have victory in our lives. Jesus is an omnipresent invisible Spirit, who will manifest His presence and transform us to be more like Him, when we gather together in His name:

> Jesus said, *"For where two or three are gathered together in my name, there am I in the midst of them" (Matthew 18:20).*

> Paul wrote, *"Where the Spirit of the Lord is, there is liberty. But we all, with open face beholding as in a glass the glory of the Lord, are changed into the same image from glory to glory, even as by the Spirit of the Lord" (2 Corinthians 3:17-18).*

No matter what power of darkness comes against us or tries to hinder us, as we *"Fight the good fight of faith" (1 Timothy 6:12)* and put on the whole armor of God, God will give us victory:

"Finally, my brethren, be strong in the Lord, and in the power of his might. Put on the whole armour of God, that ye may be able to stand against the wiles of the devil. For we wrestle not against flesh and blood, but against principalities, against powers, against the rulers of the darkness of this world, against spiritual wickedness in high places. Wherefore take unto you the whole armour of God, that ye may be able to withstand in the evil day, and having done all, to stand. Stand therefore, having your loins girt about with truth, and having on the breastplate of righteousness; And your feet shod with the preparation of the gospel of peace; Above all, taking the shield of faith, wherewith ye shall be able to quench all the fiery darts of the wicked. And take the helmet of salvation, and the sword of the Spirit, which is the word of God: Praying always with all prayer and supplication in the Spirit, and watching thereunto with all perseverance and supplication for all saints" (Ephesians 6:10-18).

"Who shall separate us from the love of Christ? shall tribulation, or distress, or persecution, or famine, or nakedness, or peril, or sword? As it is written, For thy sake we are killed all the day long; we are accounted as sheep for the slaughter. Nay, in all these things we are more than conquerors through him that loved us. For I am persuaded, that neither death, nor life, nor angels, nor principalities, nor powers, nor things present, nor things to come, Nor height, nor depth, nor any other creature, shall be able to separate us from the love of God, which is in Christ Jesus our Lord" (Romans 8:35-39).

"But thanks be to God, which giveth us the victory through our Lord Jesus Christ" (1 Corinthians 15:57).

Some Keys to Living a Victorious Life

I believe that living a victorious life includes both *what* we do on a daily basis and *how* we view everything, which includes our attitude and perspective on life. I certainly do not claim to have all of the answers, but I believe that these are some keys to living a victorious life:

1. **View things that come our way as God would have us to.**

   "And we know that all things work together for good to them that love God, to them who are the called according to his purpose" (Romans 8:28).

   Never forget that *not* all things are good, but *all things work together for good* to them that love God and are the called according to God's purpose. In other words, God can take something bad and use it for good. For example, someone may mistreat us, but God can use that to make us a better Christian and help develop a more Christ-like character in us.

2. **Always remember that God is keeping score.**

   "Be not deceived; God is not mocked: for whatsoever a man soweth, that shall he also reap. For he that soweth to his flesh shall of the flesh reap corruption; but he that soweth to the Spirit shall of the Spirit reap life everlasting. And let us not be weary in well doing: for in due season we shall reap, if we faint not" (Galatians 6:7-9).

   God knows everything about everyone (Hebrews 4:13; Psalm 139:1-4; Proverbs 15:3). God hears and keeps track of everything that we say and do (Matthew 10:26; 12:36). Someday, we will be rewarded by God for how we have used our God-given abilities (Matthew 25:14-30). Our greatest goal in life should be for Jesus to tell us: *"Well done, thou good and faithful servant" (Matthew 25:21).*

3. **Do everything with all of our heart to God and not to men.**

   "And whatsoever ye do, do it heartily, as to the Lord, and not unto men; Knowing that of the Lord ye shall receive the reward of the inheritance: for ye serve the Lord Christ" (Colossians 3:23-24).

We should not be half-hearted (Revelation 3:16), double-minded (James 1:8) or have mixed-up priorities (Matthew 6:24). We should not do any of our actions to "be seen of men" (Matthew 6:5; 23:5). If we do everything with all of our heart to God and not unto men, then when someone that we have put confidence in disappoints us, we will still be giving our very best to God. Others will sin, make mistakes, and periodically disappoint us, but God will *never* disappoint us.

4. Keep a clean heart and a right spirit.

"Keep thy heart with all diligence; for out of it are the issues of life" (Proverbs 4:23).

"Create in me a clean heart, O God; and renew a right spirit within me" (Psalm 51:10).

We need to maintain a spirit of forgiveness by praying for those that have mistreated us in some way:

Jesus said, *"Ye have heard that it hath been said, Thou shalt love thy neighbour, and hate thine enemy. But I say unto you, Love your enemies, bless them that curse you, do good to them that hate you, and pray for them which despitefully use you, and persecute you; That ye may be the children of your Father which is in heaven: for he maketh his sun to rise on the evil and on the good, and sendeth rain on the just and on the unjust. For if ye love them which love you, what reward have ye? do not even the publicans the same? And if ye salute your brethren only, what do ye more than others? do not even the publicans so? Be ye therefore perfect, even as your Father which is in heaven is perfect" (Matthew 5:43-48).*

Like God, we should desire for everyone to be saved (1 Timothy 2:4; 2 Peter 3:9; Ezekiel 33:11). For example, Jesus forgave others while he was dying on the cross (Luke 23:34) and God empowered Stephen to forgive others while he was being stoned to death (Acts 7:60).

5. **Do not compare ourselves with others.**

> *"For we dare not make ourselves of the number, or compare ourselves with some that commend themselves: but they measuring themselves by themselves, and comparing themselves among themselves, are not wise" (2 Corinthians 10:12).*

> *"Truly God is good to Israel, even to such as are of a clean heart. But as for me, my feet were almost gone; my steps had well nigh slipped. For I was envious at the foolish, when I saw the prosperity of the wicked" (Psalm 73:1-3).*

The members of God's Church (or "body of Christ") have a variety of different God-given abilities, offices, and gifts (Romans 12:4-8; 1 Corinthians 12:4-31; Ephesians 4:7-16). We need to: (a) Find out "where we fit" in God's body, and (b) Do our best to work in harmony with those in God's Church to reach others with our glorious message of salvation.

6. **Stay full of the Holy Ghost.** This is done by:
   a. Maintaining a consistent prayer life (Psalm 55:17; Daniel 6:10; Matthew 6:9-13; 14:23; Mark 1:35; Luke 5:16; 6:12; 18:1; 1 Corinthians 15:31; 2 Corinthians 4:16; 1 Thessalonians 5:17; Philippians 4:6; 1 Peter 5:7).
   b. Periodically fasting (Matthew 6:16-18).
   c. Living a holy and temperate life.

> *(24) Know ye not that they which run in a race run all, but one receiveth the prize? So run, that ye may obtain. (25) And every man that striveth for the mastery is temperate in all things. Now they do it to obtain a corruptible crown; but we an incorruptible. (26) I therefore so run, not as uncertainly; so fight I, not as one that beateth the air: (27) But I keep under my body, and bring it into subjection: lest that by any means, when I have preached to others, I myself should be a castaway" (1 Corinthians 9:24-27).*

The words "striveth for the mastery" (1 Corinthians 9:25, KJV) are translated as "competes for the prize" (NKJV). We can *all* be a winner in this race. Being "temperate in all things" is simply exercising self-control in all of our personal habits.

7. Hide the Word of God in our heart.

> *"Only be thou strong and very courageous, that thou mayest observe to do according to all the law, which Moses my servant commanded thee: turn not from it to the right hand or to the left, that thou mayest prosper whithersoever thou goest. This book of the law shall not depart out of thy mouth; but thou shalt meditate therein day and night, that thou mayest observe to do according to all that is written therein: for then thou shalt make thy way prosperous, and then thou shalt have good success. Have not I commanded thee? Be strong and of a good courage; be not afraid, neither be thou dismayed: for the LORD thy God is with thee whithersoever thou goest"* *(Joshua 1:7-9).*

> *"Blessed is the man that walketh not in the counsel of the ungodly, nor standeth in the way of sinners, nor sitteth in the seat of the scornful. But his delight is in the law of the LORD; and in his law doth he meditate day and night. And he shall be like a tree planted by the rivers of water, that bringeth forth his fruit in his season; his leaf also shall not wither; and whatsoever he doeth shall prosper"* *(Psalm 1:1-3).*

> *"Thy word have I hid in mine heart, that I might not sin against thee"* *(Psalm 119:11).*

> *"Thy word is a lamp unto my feet, and a light unto my path"* *(Psalm 119:105).*

> *"But sanctify the Lord God in your hearts: and be ready always to give an answer to every man that asketh you a reason of the hope that is in you with meekness and fear"* *(1 Peter 3:15).*

We should read the Bible (Scriptures) daily (Acts 17:11). Jesus, who was our example in all things, used the Scriptures to defend himself when he was tempted by the devil (Matthew 4:1-11). We should also use *"The sword of the Spirit, which is the word of God"* *(Ephesians 6:17)*, to defend ourselves when we are tempted.

8. Think on good things.

"Finally, brethren, whatsoever things are true, whatsoever things are honest, whatsoever things are just, whatsoever things are pure, whatsoever things are lovely, whatsoever things are of good report; if there be any virtue, and if there be any praise, think on these things. Those things, which ye have both learned, and received, and heard, and seen in me, do: and the God of peace shall be with you" *(Philippians 4:8-9).*

Jesus said, *"I will never leave thee, nor forsake thee. So that we may boldly say, the Lord is my helper, and I will not fear what man shall do unto me"* *(Hebrews 13:5-6).*

"There hath no temptation taken you but such as is common to man: but God is faithful, who will not suffer you to be tempted above that ye are able; but will with the temptation also make a way to escape, that ye may be able to bear it" *(1 Corinthians 10:13).*

"God is our refuge and strength, a very present help in trouble" *(Psalm 46:1).*

"The LORD will give grace and glory: no good thing will he withhold from them that walk uprightly" *(Psalm 84:11).*

Jesus *"is a friend that sticketh closer than a brother"* *(Proverbs 18:24).*

"For I reckon that the sufferings of this present time are not worthy to be compared with the glory which shall be revealed in us" *(Romans 8:18).*

Remember that each day is a gift from God:

"This is the day which the LORD hath made; we will rejoice and be glad in it" *(Psalms 118:24).*

"Blessed be the Lord, who daily loadeth us with benefits, even the God of our salvation" *(Psalm 68:19).*

"It is of the LORD's mercies that we are not consumed, because his compassions fail not. They are new every morning: great is thy faithfulness" *(Lamentations 3:22-23).*

Do not be focused on the past, but instead, be looking forward to the future:

> *"Brethren, I count not myself to have apprehended: but this one thing I do, forgetting those things which are behind, and reaching forth unto those things which are before, I press toward the mark for the prize of the high calling of God in Christ Jesus." (Philippians 3:13-14).*

The word "before" (Philippians 3:13, KJV) is translated as "ahead" (NKJV).

9. Encourage yourself and rejoice in your God.

> *"And David was greatly distressed; for the people spake of stoning him, because the soul of all the people was grieved, every man for his sons and for his daughters: but David encouraged himself in the LORD his God"*
> *(1 Samuel 30:6).*

> *"Why art thou cast down, O my soul? and why art thou disquieted within me? hope thou in God: for I shall yet praise him, who is the health of my countenance, and my God" (Psalm 42:11).*

> *"Although the fig tree shall not blossom, neither shall fruit be in the vines; the labour of the olive shall fail, and the fields shall yield no meat; the flock shall be cut off from the fold, and there shall be no herd in the stalls: Yet I will rejoice in the LORD, I will joy in the God of my salvation. The LORD God is my strength" (Habakkuk 3:17-19).*

Even in discouraging circumstances or situations, we must learn the principle of encouraging ourself and rejoicing in our God. God is faithful (1 Thessalonians 5:24) and will never disappoint us (Hebrews 13:5-6).

10. Maintain a spirit of thanksgiving to God.
Jesus healed ten men that were lepers (Luke 17:12-15). Jesus was disappointed that only one of the ten men came back to Jesus and gave thanks (Luke 17:15-19).

> *"In every thing give thanks: for this is the will of God in Christ Jesus concerning you" (1 Thessalonians 5:18).*

136

"Because that, when they knew God, they glorified him not as God, neither were thankful; but became vain in their imaginations, and their foolish heart was darkened" *(Romans 1:21).*

"Now when Daniel knew that the writing was signed, he went into his house; and his windows being open in his chamber toward Jerusalem, he kneeled upon his knees three times a day, and prayed, and gave thanks before his God, as he did aforetime" *(Daniel 6:10).*

"Be careful for nothing; but in every thing by prayer and supplication with thanksgiving let your requests be made known unto God. And the peace of God, which passeth all understanding, shall keep your hearts and minds through Christ Jesus" *(Philippians 4:6-7).*

11. **Do what is right in God's eyes, love mercy, and walk humbly with your God.** God said, *"But to this man will I look, even to him that is poor and of a contrite spirit, and trembleth at my word"* *(Isaiah 66:2).* The word "poor" (Isaiah 66:2, KJV) is translated as "humble" (NIV).

    "He hath shewed thee, O man, what is good; and what doth the LORD require of thee, but to do justly, and to love mercy, and to walk humbly with thy God?" *(Micah 6:8).*

    "Providing for honest things, not only in the sight of the Lord, but also in the sight of men" *(2 Corinthians 8:21).*

    "For he shall have judgment without mercy, that hath shewed no mercy; and mercy rejoiceth against judgment" *(James 2:13).*

    "Be clothed with humility: for God resisteth the proud, and giveth grace to the humble" *(1 Peter 5:5).*

    "Thus saith the LORD, Let not the wise man glory in his wisdom, neither let the mighty man glory in his might, let not the rich man glory in his riches: But let him that glorieth glory in this, that he understandeth and knoweth me, that I am the LORD which exercise lovingkindness, judgment, and righteousness, in the earth: for in these things I delight, saith the LORD" *(Jeremiah 9:23-24).*

12. Endure or persevere to the very end, regardless of whatever comes your way.

> *"And ye shall be hated of all men for my name's sake: but he that endureth to the end shall be saved" (Matthew 10:22).*

> Paul said, *"I have fought a good fight, I finished my course, I have kept the faith" (2 Timothy 4:7).*

Victory Through Jesus

I believe it is important for us to understand that God has given us everything that we need to live a victorious life. As we continue to look to Jesus, the author and finisher of our faith (Philippians 1:6; Hebrews 12:1-2), God will do whatever it takes (Ephesians 3:20) to preserve us (2 Timothy 4:18) and keep us (Jude 24):

> *"Being confident of this very thing, that he which hath begun a good work in you will perform it until the day of Jesus Christ" (Philippians 1:6).*

> *"Wherefore seeing we also are compassed about with so great a cloud of witnesses, let us lay aside every weight, and the sin which doth so easily beset us, and let us run with patience the race that is set before us, Looking unto Jesus the author and finisher of our faith" (Hebrews 12:1-2).*

> *"Now unto him that is able to do exceeding abundantly above all that we ask or think, according to the power that worketh in us" (Ephesians 3:20).*

> *"And the Lord shall deliver me from every evil work, and will preserve me unto his heavenly kingdom: to whom be glory for ever and ever. Amen" (2 Timothy 4:18).*

> *"Now unto him that is able to keep you from falling, and to present you faultless before the presence of his glory with exceeding joy" (Jude 24).*

<u>Conclusion</u>

Jesus said, *"Again, the kingdom of heaven is like unto treasure hid in a field; the which when a man hath found, he hideth, and for joy thereof goeth and selleth all that he hath, and buyeth that field" (Matthew 13:44).*

I thank God for sparing my soul and for allowing me to be a part of His blood-bought Church. The truth and *conversion experience* that I have been blessed to see and receive is something extremely *precious* to me. Words cannot properly describe how completely awesome it is to have God fill you with His Spirit and establish a permanent residence in your inner man. He totally transforms your priorities and the way that you think. He really puts a desire in you to make your life count for His cause. I had never experienced such love, joy, and peace in my innermost being. I did my best to "sell out" and buy that "treasure-filled field" many years ago and it is truly the best deal that I ever received. I am forever grateful to those that took time to be a real friend to me and explain to me the New Testament plan of salvation in the Bible.

I have had a deep love for Jesus since I was twenty-five years old and Jesus has always been so kind and good to me. He is truly a friend that loveth at all times and a friend that sticketh closer than a brother. He is a very present help in any time of need. I love serving God and feel very indebted to such a totally wonderful and marvelous God. I count it a high privilege and honor to be called out of darkness into His marvelous light. Ever since I became a member of God's New Testament Church, God has stirred me up to want to talk to others about all that He has done in my life. The "Spirit of Christ" dwelling in me (Romans 8:9) has wanted me to glorify God in all that I do and say.

My prayer is that whoever reads this book would somehow be open to all that was said. I truly believe that what I have experienced and received from God is something that God wants for everyone.

Endnotes

[1]Vine, W. E., M. A. Entry for 'Lord'. *Vine's Expository Dictionary of OT Words.* <https://www.studylight.org/dictionaries/eng/vot/l/lord.html.> 1940. Accessed 4 Oct. 2022.

[2]Vine, W. E., M. A. Entry for 'Jesus'. *Vine's Expository Dictionary of NT Words.* <https://www.studylight.org/dictionaries/eng/ved/j/jesus.html.> 1940. Accessed 4 Oct. 2022.

[3]Clarke, Adam. "Commentary on 2 Corinthians 5:19." *The Adam Clarke Commentary.* <https://www.studylight.org/commentaries/eng/acc/2-corinthians-5.html.> 1832. Accessed 19 Oct. 2022.

[4]Vines, W. E., M. A. Entry for 'Gospel'. *Vine's Expository Dictionary of NT Words.* <https://www.studylight.org/dictionaries/eng/ved/g/ gospel.html.> 1940. Accessed 4 Oct. 2022.

[5]Matthew 27:26 footnote on "Flogged" *Holman Christian Standard Bible®* Copyright © 1999, 2000, 2002, 2003, 2005 by Holman Bible Publishers.

[6]Vine, W. E., M. A. Entry for 'Scourge'. *Vine's Expository Dictionary of NT Words.* <https://www.studylight.org/dictionaries/eng/ved/s/scourge.html.> 1940. Accessed 4 Oct. 2022.

[7]Vine, W. E., M. A. Entry for 'Redeem, Redemption'. *Vine's Expository Dictionary of NT Words.* <https://www.studylight.org/dictionaries/eng /ved/r/redeem-redemption.html.> 1940. Accessed 4 Oct. 2022.

[8]Ibid., Entry for 'Buy, Bought'. Accessed 4 Oct. 2022.

[9]"Redeem." *Webster's 1913 Online Dictionary,* <https://www.websters1913.com/words/Redeem>. Accessed 29 Sep. 2022.

[10]Vine, W. E., M. A. Entry for 'Reconcile, Reconciliation'. *Vine's Expository Dictionary of NT Words.* <https://www.studylight.org/ dictionaries /eng/ved/r/reconcile-reconciliation.html.> 1940. Accessed 4 Oct. 2022.

[11]"Reconcile." *Webster's 1913 Online Dictionary,* <https://www. websters1913.com/words/Reconcile>. Accessed 29 Sep. 2022.

[12]Clarke, Adam. "Commentary on Exodus 23:14." *The Adam Clarke Commentary.* <https://www.studylight.org/commentaries/eng/acc/exodus-23.html.> 1832. Accessed 19 Oct. 2022.

[13]F.F. Bruce, *Paul: Apostle of the Heart Set Free,* (Grand Rapids, Mi.: William B. Eerdmans Publishing Company, 1977), p. 174.

[14]Ibid., p. 444.

[15]Ibid., p. 475.

[16]Vine, W. E., M. A. Entry for 'Fear'. *Vine's Expository Dictionary of OT Words.* <https://www.studylight.org/dictionaries/eng/vot/f/fear.html.> 1940. Accessed 4 Oct. 2022.

[17]Ibid., Entry for 'Forsake'. Accessed 4 Oct. 2022.

[18]Vine, W. E., M. A. Entry for 'Right, Right Hand, Right Side'. *Vine's Expository Dictionary of NT Words.* <https://www.studylight.org/dictionaries /eng/ved/r/right-right-hand-right-side.html.> 1940. Accessed 4 Oct. 2022.

Bibliography

Bernard, David. *Spiritual Gifts*. Hazelwood, Mo.:
Word Aflame Press, 1997.

Bernard, David. *The Message of Romans*. Hazelwood, Mo.:
Word Aflame Press, 1987.

Bernard, David. *The New Birth*. Hazelwood, Mo.:
Word Aflame Press, 1984.

Bernard, David. *The Oneness of God*. Hazelwood, Mo.:
Word Aflame Press, 2001.

Bruce, F.F. *Paul: Apostle of the Heart Set Free*. Grand Rapids,
Mi.: William B. Eerdmans Publishing Company, 1977.

Clarke, Adam. *The Adam Clarke Commentary*. 1832.

Coon, Crawford D. *Christian Development Course Volume I - A Reason of the Hope*. Hazelwood, Mo.: Word Aflame Press,
1987.

Erickson, Gary. *The Conversion Experience*. Hazelwood, MO:
Word Aflame Press, 1987.

Graves, Robert Brent. *The God of Two Testaments*. 1977.

Hall, J. L., and David K. Bernard, editors. *Doctrines of the Bible*.
Hazelwood, Mo.: Word Aflame Press, 1993.

Haney, Kenneth. *Baptism of Fire*, Stockton, CA, 2001.

Jensen, Irving. *Acts: A Self-Study Guide*. Moody Bible Institute
of Chicago, 1969.

Kinzie, Fred. *Handbook on Receiving the Holy Ghost*. Hazelwood,
Mo.: Word Aflame Press, 1997.

Kinzie, Fred. *Salvation in the Book of Acts*. Hazelwood, Mo.:
Word Aflame Press, 1988.

Holy Bible, The, King James Version.

Holy Bible, New International Version. Grand Rapids:
Zondervan, 2011.

Holy Bible, The, New King James Version. Nashville: Thomas
Nelson Publishers, 1982.

Kinsey, Brian. *The Bride's Pearl, A Commentary on Ephesians*.
Hazelwood, MO. Word Aflame Press. 1993.

Nave, Orville J. *Nave's Topical Bible: A Digest of the Holy Scriptures*. Peabody, MA: Hendrickson Publishers, 1997.

Reynolds, Ralph. *Dividing the Word of Truth*. Alpha Bible Publications, 2016.

Reynolds, Ralph. *Truth Shall Triumph*. Hazelwood, Mo.: Word Aflame Press, 2007.

Seagraves, Daniel. *First Peter: Standing Fast in the Grace of God*. Hazelwood, MO. Word Aflame Press, 1999.

Seagraves, Daniel. *Hebrews: Better Things, Volume One A Commentary on Hebrews 1-8*. Hazelwood, MO. Word Aflame Press, 1996.

Seagraves, Daniel. *Living By Faith: A Verse-by-Verse Study of Romans*. Kearney, NE. Morris Publishing, 2000.

Seagraves, Daniel. *Second Peter & Jude*. Hazelwood, MO. Word Aflame Press, 2000.

Smith, Larry. *Rightly Dividing the Word*. El Campo, TX, 1979.

Smith, Larry. *The Godhead*. El Campo, TX, 1982.

Strong, James. *Exhaustive Concordance of the Bible*. Nashville: Abingdon, 1890.

The Amplified Bible: Containing the Amplified Old Testament and the Amplified New Testament. Grand Rapids, MI: Zondervan Publishing House, 1987.

Vine, W. E. *Vine's Expository Dictionary of NT Words*. 1940

Vine, W. E. *Vine's Expository Dictionary of OT Words*. 1940

"Water Baptism in Scripture and History". Hazelwood, Mo.: Word Aflame Press, 2013.

Webster, Noah. *Webster's 1913 Online Dictionary*. edited by Noah Porter, Springfield, MA. G. & C. Merriam Co., 1913.

Made in the USA
Columbia, SC
09 October 2024

43381200R00089